To
_____

From
_____

Date
_____

Morning Gratitude

INSPIRING MOMENTS *to* START YOUR DAY

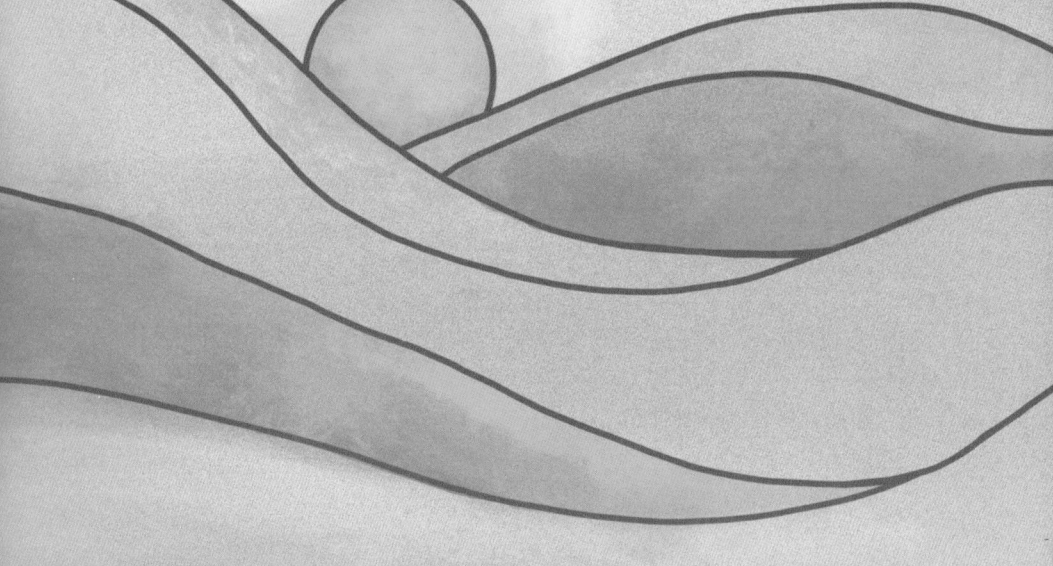

PRAY.COM

Morning Gratitude: Inspiring Moments to Start Your Day.
Copyright 2023 Pray.com, All rights reserved.
First edition, October 2023

Published by:

21154 Highway 16 East
Siloam Spring, AR 72761
dayspring.com

All rights reserved. *Morning Gratitude: Inspiring Moments to Start Your Day* is under copyright protection. No part of this book may be used or reproduced in any manner whatsoever without written permission except in the case of brief quotations embodied in critical articles and reviews.

Scriptures marked NIV are taken from the Holy Bible, New International Version®, NIV®. Copyright © 1973, 1978, 1984, 2011 by Biblica, Inc.® Used by permission of Zondervan. All rights reserved worldwide. www.zondervan.com. The "NIV" and "New International Version" are trademarks registered in the United States Patent and Trademark Office by Biblica, Inc.®

Scripture quotations marked ESV are taken from the ESV Bible® (The Holy Bible, English Standard Version®) copyright ©2001 by Crossway Bibles, a publishing ministry of Good News Publishers. Used by permission. All rights reserved..

Scripture quotations marked NLT are taken from the Holy Bible, New Living Translation, copyright © 1996, 2004, 2015 by Tyndale House Foundation. Used by permission of Tyndale House Publishers, Inc., Carol Stream, Illinois 60188. All rights reserved.

Scripture quotations marked KJV taken from the Holy Bible, King James Version.

Scripture quotations marked CEV are from the Contemporary English Version Copyright © 1991, 1992, 1995 by American Bible Society, Used by Permission.

Scripture quotations marked NCV are from the New Century Version®. Copyright © 2005 by Thomas Nelson, Inc. Used by permission. All rights reserved.

Scripture quotations marked AMP are taken from the Amplified Bible, Copyright © 2015 by The Lockman Foundation. Used by permission.

Scripture quotations marked THE MESSAGE are taken from THE MESSAGE, copyright © 1993, 1994, 1995, 1996, 2000, 2001, 2002 by Eugene H. Peterson. Used by permission of NavPress. All rights reserved. Represented by Tyndale House Publishers, Inc.

Written by: Pray.com
Additional content collaboration provided by: Christy Phillippe
Cover Design by: Becca Barnett and Brady Voss

Printed in China
Prime: U1298
ISBN: 979-8-88602-437-1

Note to the Reader

You've likely picked up this book because you desire a connection with God. Learning to talk and pray with God tethers our hearts to His. However, the idea of praying can be daunting at times. It can feel confusing and raise questions like: What should I say? What does God even want me to pray about? Where do I start? Let this devotional be a guide for you. Throughout this book, you will explore different topics to facilitate conversations between you and your Creator. You'll learn to talk with Him about anxiety, depression, grace, love, fear, and doubt. Rest assured; no topic is too difficult for God. Talking with Him regularly will give you a deep connection to His heart.

These daily devotions will encourage you to find a quiet and meaningful space to talk with God regularly. And it is our hope that in these tender moments, your prayer life will be shaped in a way that brings you closer to God and deepens your relationship with Him.

Within the following pages, you'll find prayers and inspirations that focus on ten main themes: grounding in love, releasing anger, processing through anxiety, understanding grief, walking through depression, living in transformation, sleeping peacefully, pursuing plans, leading in a Christ-like manner, and receiving the grace of God.

Regardless of where you stand in your spiritual journey, our intention with this book is to guide you towards aligning your heart with the promises of God, fostering a profound and meaningful connection between you and your Creator. May your reading experience be immersed in the boundless love and profound peace that is only found in the presence of God.

Contents

Note to the Reader.................... 5
God's Peace........................... 8
Let Go of Perfection 10
Cultivating Humility................ 12
Self-Control in Relationships 14
Negotiating Sticky Situations...... 16
Practicing Kindness and Humility . 18
The Power of Your Words 20

SECTION: MORNING GRATITUDE

Choose Joy 22
From Weakness to Strength 24
Trusting God Despite Fear 26
Gratitude in Difficulties............ 28
Seeking God Requires Faith........ 30
Wholehearted Praise 32
Live for God Always 34

SECTION: LETTING GO

Trusting God in All Things.......... 36
True Freedom...................... 38
Letting Go of Unforgiveness 40
The Mercies of God 42
Letting Go of Fear 44
Your Identity in Christ............. 46
Letting Go of the Past.............. 48

SECTION: DEEP FORGIVENESS

God Commands Forgiveness....... 50
Limitless Forgiveness............... 52
Sow Forgiveness,
Harvest Blessings.................. 54

Love As Jesus Loved 56
Overcoming Evil with Good 58
Kindness Overcomes Evil......... 60
God's Justice and Forgiveness...... 62

SECTION: NEW FRIENDSHIPS

Covenant Friendships 64
The Blessing of Friendship 66
Steadfast Friends................... 68
Practicing Empathy................ 70
Being Accountable 72
Interceding for Your Friends 74
True Selflessness 76

SECTION: MORE PRODUCTIVITY

Purposeful Creation 78
Committing to God's Blessing 80
Focusing on God................... 82
Consider the Ant 84
Using Time Wisely................. 86
Carpe Diem!....................... 88
Productivity Brings Joy 90

SECTION: REST AND RECOVER

Entering God's Rest................ 92
God's Presence Brings Rest 94
Gratitude Brings Rest.............. 96
Restoration from the Lord 98
Serving Others 100
Provision through Prayer 102
The Lord Refreshes My Soul...... 104

SECTION: POSITIVE MINDSET

Godly Positivity 106
Choose a Godly Mindset 108
Fill Your Mind with the Word 110
Assurance in God 112
God Is Enough 114
Speaking Life 116
God-Given Power 118

SECTION: STAYING ON TRACK

Putting God First 120
Watch What You Do 122
Seek God First 124
Perseverance 126
Behave Yourself! 128
Find Your Strength in God 130
No Turning Back 132

SECTION: SPIRITUAL FITNESS

Spiritual Well-Being 134
Constant Transformation 136
Walking in God's
Calling and Purpose 138
Constant Vigilance 140
Walking in the Spirit 142
Your Body Is a Holy Offering 144
Your Spiritual Health 146

SECTION: BECOMING PRESENT

God's Progressive Work 148
Entrusting Your Future to God 150
True Contentment 152
Seek Him First 154

Great Things Ahead! 156
Maintaining Joy 158
Our Constant, Unchanging God . . . 160

SECTION: SUSTAINED FAITH

True Belief in God 162
How Faith Comes 164
Meeting God through Our Faith . . . 166
Pleasing God through Our Faith . . . 168
Faith Brings Healing 170
Persevere in Your Faith 172
God Increases Faith 174

SECTION: CONQUER LONELINESS

God Loves You! 176
God Will Never Abandon You 178
Call Upon God 180
God's Unconditional Love 182
Our Covenant-Keeping God 184
Receiving Hope 186
Never Alone 188

SECTION: ENJOYING LIFE

God Has Good Things for You! 190
Keeping Priorities Straight 192
Overtaken with Blessings 194
Living a Prosperous Life 196
Safe and Protected 198
Run Your Race in Faith 200
Identity and Purpose 202
Giving Thanks in All Things 204
God's Great Love 206

God's Peace

"Blessed are the peacemakers:
for they shall be called the children of God."

MATTHEW 5:9 KJV

While relationships can sometimes be difficult, we can be grateful that God has provided His peace for our lives—and He says that His peace surpasses all our human understanding could ever comprehend. Peace with God and peace with others—that is what His Spirit can bring to our lives as we ask Him into our relationships. When other people are unkind, when they say or do things that upset you, that break your trust or even your heart, being a peacemaker, as Jesus asks, may seem impossible. But when you confess to the Lord all your hurt, all your anger, and all your pain, He will come into your heart and help you to forgive, to live in peace with Him, with others, and even with yourself.

What blessings of peace have you enjoyed? What relationships has God restored in your life? Think of the delight that has come into your heart because of peace. In what past situations did you reach out to turn anger into agreement? With an attitude of gratitude, thank the Lord for helping you resolve past conflicts and for the fruits of joy and growth that have come from those relationships. Thank Him for the times you spend free from fear and hostility. And thank Him for the future reconciliation in your current broken relationships.

Remember that God has called you to be a peacemaker. He wants you, as far as it is possible for you, to live as a peacemaker, bringing restoration and calm to all places where there is discord and disagreement. As you work toward living amicably and in unity with everyone you can, God will also work peace into your soul and spirit. Through obedience to God's Word and a desire to bring harmony to all your relationships, you can become a peacemaker!

God is present today, and He is listening to you as you pray for peace in every area of your life. Thank Him for His help and the ability to resolve conflicts. Ask Him for creative solutions to mend old bridges and build new ones, connecting people with each other and with God. Pray for peace in all your interactions; peace with your family and friends; peace at work with your superiors and your colleagues; peace in every area, every aspect, and every relationship in your life. And give thanks to God when He brings it to pass.

PRAYER

God, I praise You for Your peace, which surpasses all understanding. Your peace overcomes all circumstances, all fear and doubts. God, I worship You for giving me the ability to be a peacemaker. I praise You for calling me Your child. I know that You love me and that You have already provided a resolution to all conflict. Amen.

Let Go of Perfection

Love prospers when a fault is forgiven,
but dwelling on it separates close friends.

PROVERBS 17:9 NLT

Being perfect is impossible. No human being can ever be the perfect friend, the perfect partner, the perfect person. But even though we ourselves are not perfect, we often require perfection from others. Even the people who love you the most and are the closest to you will sometimes hurt you. The Bible teaches us that everyone has sinned and fallen short of the glory of God.

With what relationships are you struggling today? Are there any that need to be repaired or restored? One way to help this process along is to let go of the perfection that many of us require and remember how much God has forgiven us for ourselves. God has not expected perfection from you—just for you to try your best.

With a heart filled with gratitude, consider all the times when God's love covered your own sins—and thank Him for it! Thank Him for forgiving all the bad stuff in your life, all the wrong choices and bad decisions that were made. Thank God for choosing to love you instead of holding your mistakes against you. Thank Him for forgiving you of all your past sins and transgressions. Give thanks to God because through His own love, He grants us the power to love others.

As you continue to thank Him for His help and guidance in your relationships, come before Him and ask Him for the strength to choose love over holding a grudge. Ask Him for help in letting go of the hurt from all the past times when someone offended you or did things that wounded you. Ask the Holy Spirit to empower you to love others the way that Jesus Himself loves them. With the ability to choose love over hurt, you will cultivate a love so great it will overcome all the wrongs that people have done to you. That doesn't mean the wrongs didn't happen, but you can choose to let it go and love the person instead. Choose to allow your love—God's love within you—to be greater than the hurt done to you, and then thank the Lord for the power and the strength to follow through.

PRAYER

God, I praise You because Your love never fails, and it covers all of my transgressions. I adore You because You are good, You are kind, and Your mercies endure forever. I praise You for Your endless grace. I worship You because You are great; there is no one else like You. I am so grateful You do not require perfection from me, that Your love covers a mountain of offenses. Help me as I seek to love others the way You love me. Amen.

Cultivating Humility

Don't be selfish; don't try to impress others.
Be humble, thinking of others as better than yourselves.

PHILIPPIANS 2:3 NLT

To think of others as better than yourself can, at times, seem arduous, annoying, and difficult. Each of us is, after all, only human, and it is in our very nature to be selfish and filled with pride. We are susceptible to acting out in anger, to being belligerent when we feel backed into a corner. Nevertheless, God has called us to be the better person in our relationships, to selflessly share His love with others, the kind of love that caused Jesus to choose the cross on our behalf. The standard set before us is high, but we can rise to the occasion.

Although you may often fail in your attempts toward humility, don't give up. God is faithful, even when we are not. The Holy Spirit stands ready to help you and enable you to accomplish this herculean task. When you set your mind to treat others as better than yourself and give others the benefit of the doubt, your relationships will not only be saved, but they will flourish.

With God's help, you can choose not to react in anger or pride. You can be the better person. You can put others higher than yourself. With the Holy Spirit's assistance, and in God's love and through His grace, you can infuse your words and actions with humility and treat others with respect and kindness, no matter how they treat you—good or bad. As you allow God to use you to be the good you want to see in the world, thank Him for working through you to restore relationships and practice love through humility in each interaction today.

> **PRAYER**
>
> *Jesus, I thank You for the fact that even though You are God, You did not hold tightly to the claim that You are equal with Your Father. Instead, in humility, You chose the cross and died on my behalf. Lord, I am so thankful that You are present and listening to me today. The Bible says that if I ask, it will be given to me, and so I ask You today for humility in my relationships. I want to be a person who treats others with the utmost respect and kindness, to put others before myself. Even if others hurt me or hinder my goals, I commit to my choice to be the better person, because You have made the way possible for me. Teach me Your humility and free me from my pride, I pray. Thank You for helping me to succeed in this important task. Amen.*

Self-Control in Relationships

My dear friends,
you should be quick to listen
and slow to speak or to get angry.

JAMES 1:19 CEV

As believers, we are called to live a life that is pleasing to God. Part of that involves being willing to listen, being careful with our words, and controlling our emotions. However, this is not always easy, especially in a world that can be unpredictable and chaotic.

We are constantly bombarded with situations that can provoke, aggravate, and grieve us. Sometimes, we may be tempted to lash out in anger or say things that we will later regret. This is where relying on the Holy Spirit becomes crucial.

The Holy Spirit is our helper, our guide, and our comforter. He is always ready and willing to assist us in controlling our emotions and our words. We need to lift up to God those emotions that seem to get the best of us and be honest with ourselves and with God in prayer.

Reflecting on past experiences where God has helped us exercise self-control can be a great encouragement. We should thank God for all the past relationships where we were a blessing to others and think of all the areas we want to improve in and thank God for the growth to come.

Having control is not effortless, but it is obtainable. God never said we wouldn't feel anger, but He gave us the ability to control it. We should always be willing to listen, think things through before we speak, and not easily become mad. These simple principles, when applied in our lives, can help our relationships to flourish.

We must trust in God and in the power and promises of His Word. We should ask the Holy Spirit to bear His fruit in our lives: love, joy, peace, patience, kindness, goodness, faithfulness, gentleness, and self-control.

So let us be bold and ask the Holy Spirit to help us control our emotions, have compassion and interest when others are sharing, consider our words before we speak, and not let the actions of others control our own. Remember, God is in our corner, cheering us on.

PRAYER

Heavenly Father, I thank You that You are real and that You hear me; that You have given me the ability to practice self-control; that You love me and are concerned about my life and my relationships. I praise You for giving me wisdom and for molding my character to make me more like Your Son, Jesus. You have called me to greater things and a higher purpose. I thank You that through Christ, who strengthens me, I can do anything You ask. Amen.

Negotiating Sticky Situations

Be completely humble and gentle;
be patient, bearing with one another in love.

EPHESIANS 4:2 NIV

Loving others in meekness and through longsuffering is undoubtedly a high goal to achieve. However, as we journey through life, we will encounter people who are difficult to deal with, leading to relationships that were once secure becoming minefields. In such situations, navigating without a detonation can be challenging.

The solution lies in relying on the help of the Holy Spirit, who was designed by God to help us be more like Jesus, humble and gentle, and to help us put up with each other in patience and love. Reflecting on recent situations where our actions lacked humility, patience, and love can lead us to confess to God for redemption and restoration.

It is essential to remember that God's love for us will never fail. His patience is eternal, and nothing will ever separate us from His love. Therefore, we must thank God for His love and consider past experiences where He used others to show us love through patience and gentleness. In turn, we should strive to love others through the same.

God wants us not only to succeed but also to thrive and have happy and healthy relationships. He died to give us the power to overcome sin and live according to His Word. Therefore, it's crucial to reach out to God for guidance and ask the Holy Spirit to help us relate to the people around us in love.

As God instructs us to bear with one another in love through humility, gentleness, and patience, our aim should be to sustain unity and peace. We should be encouraged because we are not alone in this mission. The Holy Spirit is always there to help us and guide us. He will never leave or abandon us—and because of Him, we can do this.

We strive to love others in meekness and through longsuffering, relying on the help of the Holy Spirit. By doing so, we can maintain happy and healthy relationships while promoting unity and peace.

PRAYER

God, I worship You for who You are. I will love You with all my heart, with all my soul, and with all my might. For You who knew no sin became sin so that I might become the righteousness of God. Your power is infinite, yet You oppose the proud and give grace to the humble. Before the foundations of the earth were established, You called me by my name. You alone are worthy to be praised! Amen.

Practicing Kindness and Humility

We should try to live at peace and
help each other have a strong faith.

ROMANS 14:19 CEV

Trying to ensure that your actions lead to general peace and improvement can be quite daunting. It can seem like an impossible task when you have inner conflicts, personal problems, and staggering struggles to solve. However, God expects you to care for others and be courteous to them, even when you are going through difficulties yourself.

Sometimes, the pressure can be too much to bear, and you may feel like giving up. But don't lose heart; instead, lay it all at the feet of Jesus. Confess your concerns to Him and cast your burdens upon Him, knowing that He cares for you.

Take a moment to reflect on the peace and guidance that God has provided in your life. Think about the seasons of turmoil and insecurity that He has brought you through and the relationships He has helped you renew. Remember that God is good, and His mercy endures from generation to generation.

Think about the areas of life that you are trying to improve, the relationships and situations that you are trying to bring peace to and edify. Envision God's provision for those circumstances and thank Him for it. Believe that God is present and listening to you, and that He will give you the strength to reach your full potential and inspire others to do the same.

Remember that God has called you to bring peace and to inspire edification. Although it may be tough, God has already provided all that you need to accomplish this task. Be confident that God, who began a good work in you, will carry it through to completion.

As you go about your day, try your best to live in harmony with everyone and always work toward improvement. Remember to do things that not only entertain but also enlighten others. Press onward toward the goal that is Christ Jesus, and you will be a blessing to everyone you encounter.

PRAYER

Lord Jesus, I praise You because You always finish what You start. I worship You for the power of Your Word that transforms and renews my mind. I sing praises to Your name for You hold the universe in the palm of Your hand. I worship You in the knowledge that You work out all things for the good of those who love You. Amen.

The Power of Your Words

What you say can mean life or death.
Those who speak with care will be rewarded.

PROVERBS 18:21 NCV

Your words hold power, and they can have a lasting impact on the lives of those around you. With just a few words, you can either uplift someone else's spirit or bring them down.

It is important to be mindful of what we say, especially in our relationships. The way we communicate with others can either build them up or tear them down. We must strive to use our words to encourage, to heal, and to bring life to those around us. And if we do find ourselves using our words to hurt or harm others, we must take responsibility for our actions and seek forgiveness.

As we reflect on our words and their impact on our relationships, we must also take time to thank God for His words of love and encouragement spoken over us. We must ask for His help in controlling our emotions and speaking with wisdom and kindness. When we speak with love and kindness, we create an atmosphere of peace and harmony in our relationships.

We must always remember that our words hold power! We should choose them wisely and use them to bring life to those around us. Let us thank God for His words of love and encouragement spoken over us and ask for His help in using our words to uplift and encourage those around us. May we strive to create an atmosphere of peace and harmony in all our relationships, trusting in God's Word and His blessings.

> **PRAYER**
>
> *Yours, O Lord, is the greatness and the power and the glory. The majesty and the splendor of everything in heaven and on earth is Yours. Yours, Lord, are all the kingdoms of the world. You are exalted as head over all, and I will praise You all the days of my life.*

SECTION:
MORNING GRATITUDE

Choose Joy

This is the day that the Lord has made;
let us rejoice and be glad in it.

PSALM 118:24 ESV

Each day is a new beginning, an opportunity to start anew. It can be seen as a burden or as a chance to make positive changes. Your perspective will greatly impact the outcome of your day. You have the power to choose joy and happiness, even in the midst of difficulty and hardship.

Think back to the times when your choices were not optimistic, when hardship got the best of you, and when circumstances were robbing you of your daily joy. Take a moment to reflect on those moments and gather those choices, decisions, and thoughts, then place them in the hands of Jesus. Confess your feelings of sadness, discouragement, and apathy to the Lord, allowing the Holy Spirit to minister to the areas of your heart where joy does not yet reign.

Now change the script: remember the mornings filled with joy and gladness and how wonderful it felt to allow cheerfulness to prevail over discouragement. Thank God for the ability to feel gladness and to rejoice. Give thanks for the moments when happiness was greater than hopelessness, and for the blessings of past seasons of cheerfulness and contentment—and for those still yet to come. Thank Him also for the strength to choose joy—and to keep choosing it, no matter what each day may bring.

God is present and is listening to you. He desires for you to live a life filled with joy and gladness. Jesus wants to turn your sorrow into joy and your mourning into dancing. Pray for overwhelming joy that renews each day and ask the Holy Spirit to teach you to find joy even in the midst of sorrow. Ask Him to fill your heart with gladness beyond measure.

Finally, do not forget that God has called us to a life filled with joy and gladness, even in the challenges that we face. Do not be discouraged by past setbacks, as there is always a choice—and there is power in the choosing! Choose joy for today and for every day to come. Choose the joy of the Lord and watch as that joy transforms your life.

PRAYER

Lord, I praise You for this day and its possibilities, for this opportunity to love You and serve You. I praise You, the Maker of this day and all the days to come. God, I worship You for giving me the ability to be glad and to rejoice in this day. I praise You, the Creator of the heavens and the earth and everything in between. I know that You have created this day for me and given me a purpose within it. Help me to live it fully—for You. Amen.

From Weakness to Strength

*But as for me, I will sing about Your power.
Each morning I will sing with joy about Your unfailing love.
For You have been my refuge,
a place of safety when I am in distress.*

PSALM 59:16 NLT

Life can be trying and overwhelming at times. We face various obstacles and obligations that can make us feel feeble and fainthearted. We experience accusations and afflictions that continuously threaten to drown us, making it an unachievable task to keep our heads above water. It is during these moments that we need to pause and reflect on what is causing our weariness and weakness.

In such moments, the best thing we can do is to confess our areas of weakness and weariness to the Holy Spirit. We open ourselves up to God and reach out for the refuge of His reassurance. He is always listening to us, and He longs to help us in our times of need.

As we reflect on our past experiences, we thank God for being our fortress when we need His shelter and protection. We thank Him for being our safe harbor in the storm and for His power and mercy. We can be grateful for all the times when we felt weak and found shelter in Him.

Even today, we can come before God and ask Him for the strength to make it through the storm, to give us the ability to navigate the waters of this life. We can ask Him to teach us to lean on Him during times of trouble and know that He will never fail us or forsake us. We can ask the Holy Spirit to empower us to have faith in God's mercy and to remember that defense and deliverance can always be found in Him. We can ask God to teach us to seek Him as our sanctuary and stronghold, to know that He is a tower that will never shake, nor will it succumb to the waves and waters of this world.

The almighty God is our defender and protector. He is a shield that cannot be splintered or shattered, and He is the Rock on which we can stand strong. Have faith in Him, and trust in His promises this day, and in the days to come.

PRAYER

God, I praise You, for You are mighty to save. I adore You because Your mercies are renewed each and every morning. I praise You, for You are my Deliverer during my times of distress. I worship You, for You alone have power and dominion over all the earth. I give You my adoration, for You are in control over everything and every circumstance! Amen.

Trusting God Despite Fear

Each morning let me learn more
about Your love because I trust You.
I come to You in prayer,
asking for Your guidance.

PSALM 143:8 CEV

Depending on God to direct our lives is not an easy task. It requires a level of trust that can be daunting and demanding. Our human nature pushes us to seek knowledge of what is coming next, and the unknown can be frightening. But when we trust in God, we must seek His assurance over our own human nature.

It is easy to falter in our trust and allow fear and doubt to disable us. However, we can come before God with all our distrust and disbelief, telling Him about the moments when we have faltered in our faith. We put our trust in His lovingkindness and His faithfulness.

Take a few moments to dwell on the blessings that God has placed into your life in the past, and thank Him for the blessings yet to come. Through His love, you no longer need to be bound by fear, but you can operate in perpetual trust. As you seek God every morning, ask Him to guide you throughout the day, to bless the choices you make, and to give you direction.

God delights in blessing us, and He wants to give us the desires of our hearts. He calls us with lovingkindness, and we can trust in the truth of His Word. His plans for us are good—even better than we can imagine! We must not be afraid to step out of our comfort zone, instead trusting Him to guide us on the best possible path.

So today, choose to be courageous and step out into the best life that God has for you. Trust in His direction and have faith in His love toward you. With Him by your side, you can conquer any fear and overcome any obstacle that comes your way. Seek His plan for your life this day, and trust that His ways are better than your own. Continually remind yourself of His promise to prosper you, to give you hope and a future!

PRAYER

Lord, I give You praise, for Your Word is eternal. As the heavens are higher than the earth, so are Your ways higher than mine. God, Your thoughts are higher than my thoughts. I praise You because You are the everlasting God, the Creator of the ends of the earth. You do not faint or grow weary, and Your understanding is unsearchable. Thank You, Lord, for Your goodness to me! Amen.

Gratitude in Difficulties

*It is wonderful to be grateful
and to sing Your praises, LORD Most High!*

PSALM 92:1 CEV

Gratefulness is a vital aspect of our relationship with God, and it is something that we should cultivate daily. However, it can be challenging to maintain a grateful attitude when life is difficult, and we face unexpected circumstances and losses. It is in those moments that we must lift our eyes to God and trust in His goodness and love.

God never promised us an easy life, but He did promise to be with us every step of the way. He sent us the Holy Spirit to be our Helper and Guide, and we can turn to Him in prayer to ask for the strength and the courage to press on. We should be honest and open with God in prayer, confessing our hurts and struggles and asking Him to help us cultivate a grateful heart.

As we reflect on the past, we can see the evidence of God's goodness in our lives. We can recall the blessings He has poured out upon us, often undeserved and unattainable. We can remember the challenges that we thought were impossible, yet through which God made us victorious. We can look back at the moments when we thought all was lost, but God made a way where there seemed to be no way.

God is still present and listening to us today. We can ask the Holy Spirit to help us recognize God's greatness in our lives in all circumstances, even in the midst of hardship. We can thank God for all the past blessings and promises He has made to us—and for all the blessings yet to come.

Living a life filled with gratitude to God is not always easy, but it is a good thing. When we live with a thankful heart, we open ourselves up to receive the blessings that God wants to pour out on us. We can trust that God will always care for us and provide for us, and that His blessings will overflow in our lives. So, let us choose to be thankful to God every day, even in the midst of the challenges and chaos we face as we live our lives for Him.

PRAYER

Heavenly Father, I worship You for You are the God of all gods and the Lord of all lords. You are great—the mighty and awesome God over all. I praise You, for all that is in the heavens and the earth is Yours. Yours is the kingdom, O Lord, and You are exalted as Head above all. You are the King of all kings, and You are to be feared above all gods. You are great and greatly to be praised. Amen.

Seeking God Requires Faith

Lord, every morning You hear my voice.
Every morning, I tell You what I need,
and I wait for Your answer.

PSALM 5:3 NCV

When you put your trust and faith in the Lord, you can seek God's answer for your every problem and expect Him to answer your prayers. However, this requires faith—and faith is not always easy to come by. There will be times when you may find yourself lost at sea, with shredded sails and no clue how to work a winch. Fear and frustration can threaten to overwhelm you, quickly making it difficult to have faith in the midst of those difficult circumstances.

During these times, it's important to confess your doubts and fears to God. The Bible assures us that if we confess our sins, He is faithful and just to forgive us and to take the sin out of our hearts and lives. We can trust in His faithfulness—even when we are faithless.

One way to strengthen our faith is to reflect on God's faithfulness in our lives. We can thank Him for His enduring faithfulness, even when we ourselves have failed to trust Him. We can also thank Him for His Word, which is a lamp to our feet and a light to our path. When we engage with the Word of God, our faith is increased—and so are the blessings we receive!

As we seek God, though, we must remember that without faith, it is impossible to please Him. We must approach Him with the belief that He exists and that He rewards those who earnestly seek Him. We can ask the Holy Spirit to minister the truth of God's Word to our hearts, and we can trust that God will guide us through every difficult circumstance.

Because of all of this and more, let us hold tightly to our confession of hope without faltering, for the One who made His promises is faithful. We have the Holy Spirit to show us the way and to assist us in our journey of faith. So call on Jesus in boldness and expect Him not only to answer us, but to bless us beyond measure. May our faith in God be strengthened, and may we trust in His faithfulness even in the midst of life's storms.

PRAYER

God, I praise You for Your Word, which teaches us to be righteous. All Your works are done in faithfulness. I worship You, for You are not like human beings; You do not lie, nor do You change Your mind. I give You praise for You always do what You say, and what You say, You fulfill. I exalt You, Lord, for You have done wonderful things—in the world and in my own life. Amen.

Wholehearted Praise

I will praise You, Lord, with all my heart.
I will tell of all the marvelous things You have done.

PSALM 9:1 NLT

When it comes to praising God, it can be easy to get distracted and lose focus. Our hearts may want to bend under the weight of our daily lives and the pressures that come with living in this world. But if we want to praise God with our whole hearts, we commit to being fully focused on Him.

Commitment requires concentration, and the world is filled with distractions. There are constant issues and complications that are clamoring for our attention. We have deadlines and duties to attend to. At times it can seem like we are trying to carve a straight arrow from crooked wood.

The good news is that we can lay our arrow down at the feet of Jesus. We can tell Him about the knots in our hearts and the imperfections we face that keep us from praising Him with our whole hearts. We can confess our sins and cast our concerns on Christ, because He cares for us.

Take a moment to dwell on the marvelous craftmanship of God in your life. Give some thought to the wonders and miracles that God has performed for you. Thank Him for going before you and for walking beside you, for carving out your path and your future, for working out all the bumps, knots, and burls.

Remember that God has called us to praise Him with all of our hearts and to speak of His marvelous works. He cares for us and He loves us, and He has amazing and awesome adventures appointed for our lives. We cannot even begin to fathom the goodness He has in store for us.

With all these things in mind, ask the Holy Spirit to help you commit your whole heart to praising God. Allow Jesus to fill your heart with the wonder of who He is. Then, take aim and let your arrow fly! Let your whole heart soar with praise as you declare the wonders of the Lord.

PRAYER

God, I look to the skies and praise You, for You have created the stars. You lead them, and You count each one, calling each of them by name. By Your might and the strength of Your power, not one of them goes missing. I sing praises to You alone, You who do great wonders. Your path is in the whirlwind and the storm, and the clouds are the dust beneath Your feet. I worship You, for Your lovingkindness is great—above the heavens—and Your truth reaches to the skies. Amen.

Live for God Always

And whatever you do or say,
do it as a representative of the Lord Jesus,
giving thanks through Him to God the Father.

COLOSSIANS 3:17 NLT

As you go throughout the days of your life, you may find yourself waking up to a rigid schedule, or you may be greeted with a day that is free from obligations. Whatever the day ahead of you holds, you can be thankful for it. No matter what you do this day, do it for the glory of God. This is not an easy way to live—but it is the most freeing.

Consider the times in your past when your actions were unbecoming. Think of the situations when your human desires got the best of you. You must gather all your bad decisions from the past and place them in the hands of Jesus, confessing to the Lord your struggles with your human nature.

Now, think of previous days in your life that were filled with the goodness of God. Remember how it felt to act in accordance with the will of Jesus. How amazing it was to go about your day with God's presence by your side! Thank God for your relationship with Him, and share your gratitude with Him for the blessings of past seasons of goodness and accomplishment—and for those yet to come. Thank Him for current strength to make godly choices and to keep making them for the rest of your days.

Let us never forget that God is present, and He is listening to us. He desires for us to live a life of righteousness and goodness. Jesus wants to help us live each of our days according to His Word, to bless the work of our hands and to make us prosper. We must pray to Him, asking that His will be done. We must ask the Holy Spirit to teach us to seek the wisdom of the Bible, to spend time reading and understanding God's directions for a better life.

Everything you say and do should be done for Jesus. In all you do, give thanks to God the Father through Christ. Decide today to experience life in a fulfilling and satisfying way, a way in which your actions bring glory to God. Choose this day to live your life for Christ.

> **PRAYER**
>
> *Lord, I sing to You this day; I sing in praise of Your name. I extol You, who rides on the clouds! You are a Father to the fatherless, a defender of widows. You are full of goodness and righteousness. Help me to live my life this day as a worthy representation of who You are. Amen.*

SECTION:
LETTING GO

Trusting God in All Things

*For everything there is a season,
a time for every activity under heaven. . . .
A time to search and a time to quit searching.
A time to keep and a time to throw away.*

ECCLESIASTES 3:1, 6 NLT

"There is a time for everything," says the wise writer of Ecclesiastes. It's a phrase that has echoed down through the centuries, and it is still true today. Our lives are made up of different seasons, each with their own unique challenges and blessings. Whether we are experiencing joy or sorrow, victory or defeat, there is always something to be learned and gained from every season.

Yet, no matter what the season is in which we find ourselves, one thing remains constant: letting go is never easy. We all wish for more time, more opportunities to experience happiness, more chances to right wrongs and make amends. But the reality is that nothing lasts forever—except the love the Lord has for us—and there comes a time when we must let go and move on.

This can be especially difficult when we are facing sorrow or loss. The pain of saying goodbye can be overwhelming, and we may find ourselves struggling to come to terms with what has happened. But even in the midst of our grief, we can find comfort and strength in knowing that God is with us. He is present in every moment of our lives, and He has a purpose and a plan for each season we experience.

If you find yourself in a difficult season today, take heart that you are not alone. God is with you, and He will help you to let go and move on. Take this time to present yourself before Him, confess your sins, and tell Him of your struggles. Let the Holy Spirit minister to your wounded heart and teach you to trust in God's plan.

On the other hand, if you are in a season of joy and happiness, don't take it for granted! Enjoy every moment and give thanks to God for His goodness and grace. Remember that every season has its end, but that doesn't mean the end of all joy and happiness. God has a plan for your life, and He will continue to bless you in every season.

In whatever season you find yourself, choose to let go and trust in God's plan. He has a purpose for your life, and He will help you to grow and thrive in every season. Take heart—and know that God is with you always!

PRAYER

Lord God, I enter Your gates with thanksgiving and Your courts with praise. I give You thanks and magnify Your name. God, I praise You for You are good and Your love endures forever. Your faithfulness continues throughout all of time. This day, and every day, I give You glory for all Your wonderful deeds. Amen.

True Freedom

And you will know the truth [regarding salvation],
and the truth will set you free [from the penalty of sin].

JOHN 8:32 AMP

Jesus is the Truth, the only way to know the reality of life and to experience true freedom. In today's world, there are numerous sources of information, and it can be challenging to distinguish between truth and falsehood. But we must understand that truth is not an opinion or a suggestion; it is a fact that stands on its own. Truth does not cater to emotions or desires, and it is not dependent on popularity.

The truth is that Jesus is real, and His grace is enough for us. Only Jesus can give us the freedom we need to let go of all hindrances and live a life that is free from the control of sin. Therefore, it is imperative to draw near to the Truth, to draw near to Jesus, confess our sins, and ask for His forgiveness and help. We can also thank Him for all the times when He has heard our prayers, as well as for the opportunity to reach out to Him and present requests before Him.

We must never forget that God is present and listening to us. Jesus can set us free, break every chain, and take down every stronghold in our lives. The Holy Spirit can open our spiritual eyes, help us recognize truth, and empower us with godly discernment. Only then can we experience true freedom and live a life free from guilt and shame.

Jesus wants to set us free from the bondage of sin and pour out His grace and mercy upon us. He wants us to live a life free from the hindrances of sin, and it is only through Him that we can experience true freedom. So let us open our hearts to Him today and be set free. May we always seek the Truth, draw near to Jesus, and experience the freedom that only He can give!

PRAYER

Jesus, I give glory and honor to You alone, for You are the way, the truth, and the life. You pour out Your mercy and Your grace upon my life, and You set me free. Lord, I worship You, for Your power breaks every chain and destroys every stronghold of the enemy in my life. I bless Your name, Jesus, for there is none like You. Your truth, Your righteousness, and Your glory will endure forever. Amen.

Letting Go of Unforgiveness

*Stop being bitter and angry and mad at others.
Don't yell at one another or curse each other or ever be rude.
Instead, be kind and merciful, and forgive others,
just as God forgave you because of Christ.*

EPHESIANS 4:31–32 CEV

Letting go of unforgiveness is not an easy task. It requires a conscious effort to release the pain, hurt, and resentment that may have taken root in your heart. However, it is a crucial step in your spiritual growth and personal healing. Unforgiveness can eat away at your soul and rob you of the gift of being present in the moment. And it not only affects you, but it also destroys possibilities and kills relationships. Therefore, you must make the deliberate decision to forgive.

As believers, we have received God's grace and forgiveness. We are called to extend that same grace and forgiveness to others, even when it is difficult. Forgiveness is not about excusing someone's behavior or pretending that the hurt did not happen. It is about releasing the hold that the hurt has on our lives and choosing to move forward in freedom.

We can acknowledge the pain and hurt that we feel and bring it to Jesus. He understands our struggles and is willing to help us. We can ask the Holy Spirit to touch our hearts and remove any root of unforgiveness. Taking time to dwell on God's forgiveness for our own lives can also help us to extend that same forgiveness to others.

When we let go of unforgiveness, we experience a sense of freedom and peace that surpasses understanding. We become vessels of God's love and grace, allowing Him to use us to minister to others. We can be kind and loving to others, just as Christ was to us.

Choose to let go of all unforgiveness in your heart. Forgive others, as you have been forgiven by our heavenly Father. Invite the Holy Spirit to come and minister God's grace and mercy within your soul. As you do these things, you will experience the freedom and the peace that comes from living a life of forgiveness. You will become a living display of God's love and forgiveness here on the earth!

PRAYER

Jesus, I worship You for Your unending grace. I adore You, for You are the great and mighty God. Your glory cannot be hidden, Your love cannot be stopped, and Your goodness cannot be denied. Your mercy stretches across the heavens and the earth. I extol Your wonderful name, Jesus, for redemption and salvation are found in You alone. Amen.

The Mercies of God

People who conceal their sins will not prosper,
but if they confess and turn from them, they will receive mercy.

PROVERBS 28:13 NLT

Sin is a part of human nature. Everyone has, at some point, committed a sin. Sin is a deviation from God's righteousness and commands, and it creates a separation between us and God. The cost of sin is high, and it demands a price we cannot pay. However, God, in His infinite love and grace, sent His Son, Jesus Christ, to die on the cross for our sins.

God's restorative grace is freely given, but it requires acknowledgment and confession. We must acknowledge and confess our sins to God and, when necessary, to our neighbors. Covering our sins is a futile effort because God sees them anyway, and it only leads to more separation from God.

Confessing our sins to God is an opportunity to obtain mercy. We must be honest with ourselves and with God in prayer. Confession requires acknowledging and accepting our sins, forsaking them, and changing our behavior. We can then ask the Holy Spirit to cleanse our souls and wash us clean from sin. We ask Him to help us spend more time in His Word and in prayer, increase our fear and reverence for God's Word, and empower us to walk in His righteous and truthful ways.

We choose to confess our sins and reject sinning further, for in doing so, we receive God's mercy. We cannot waste our valuable time here on the earth trying to cover our sins because that only leads to more separation from God. Instead, we must choose to live a free and victorious life, empowered by the Holy Spirit, and in obedience to God's commands.

Thank God for His unending mercies and for the sacrifice of Jesus Christ, which paid the price for our salvation. Choose to confess your sins and walk in holy righteousness as the Holy Spirit empowers you to do so. May you always live a life that pleases God and brings glory to His name.

PRAYER

God, I praise You, for You are the Mighty One of Israel. I worship You, Lord, for Your mercy renews me and Your righteousness sustains me. Jesus, Your goodness is from everlasting to everlasting, and so I praise Your great name. You are my Protector and Redeemer. God, my soul trusts in You—You will never forsake me. Thank You for Your love! Amen.

Letting Go of Fear

"For I hold you by your right hand—
I, the Lord your God. And I say to you,
'Don't be afraid. I am here to help you.'"

ISAIAH 41:13 NLT

Fear can be a crippling emotion that can paralyze our lives and prevent us from experiencing the fullness of God's blessings. The enemy uses fear as a weapon to steal our joy, our peace, and our faith. However, as believers in Jesus Christ, we have the power to overcome fear and live a life of victory.

The key to overcoming fear is to let go of it and submit ourselves to God. We trust in His sovereignty and power, knowing that He is in control of all things. When we submit to God, He will fill us with the Holy Spirit, who will testify to the truth of God's Word within our hearts.

Faith is the antidote to fear, and it is the necessary weapon for us to overcome it. Faith is not just positive thinking or wishful thoughts. It is the assurance of things hoped for, the conviction of things not seen. When we place our faith in God's promises, we can overcome fear and live a life of victory.

As we reflect on our current mindset, we confess our fears to God and ask the Holy Spirit to minister to our minds and spirits. We thank God for His Holy Spirit, who casts out all fear and who ministers peace and assurance to our hearts. We ask the Holy Spirit to teach us to yield to God's commandments and be obedient to His Word.

God has not given us a spirit of fear, but of power, of love, and of a sound mind. This is a promise we can count on—it comes directly from His Word! We trust in His promises and believe that He is always with us, even in our time of need. We choose to let go of fear and live our lives boldly in the knowledge that God loves us and cares for us.

So, choose this day to let go of fear and trust in God's promises! Live your life in faith, knowing that God is with you every step of the way. Walk in victory this day, knowing that you are not alone, but that you have a God by your side who loves you and cares for you—more than you could ever know.

PRAYER

Lord, I praise You for Your unending goodness and Your constant mercy. I praise You for Your grace that You continuously pour out on my life. Your grace covers all my faults, all my sin, providing me with access to the throne room of the Father. Because of Your glorious grace, You have given me Your Holy Spirit. Thank You for these and many more blessings in my life. Amen.

Your Identity in Christ

You were told that your foolish desires will destroy you and that you must give up your old way of life with all its bad habits.

EPHESIANS 4:22 CEV

Identity is a powerful thing. It shapes the way we see ourselves and the way we interact with the world around us. Our identity determines our limitations, influences our pursuits, and ultimately impacts what we achieve. It's crucial, therefore, that we understand the importance of our identity in Christ.

Jesus calls us to let go of the pride and the vanity that hold us back, to let go of the desires of the flesh, and to stop living an ungodly lifestyle. He calls us to do this because we were created for more. We were created to live in freedom, free from the lies spoken over us, free from the limitations imposed by the shackles of corruption, and free from guilt and shame.

We can experience this freedom by embracing our true identity in Jesus Christ. We can choose to base our identity in Him. When we do this, we can experience the life-changing power of His Word, which sets us free from the bondage of sin. We can be assured of God's love for us and know that we are new creatures in Christ.

Letting go of our old identity can be challenging, but we must not give up. We must lean on God during the hard times, asking the Holy Spirit to minister to our hearts and minds, to assure us of God's love, and to empower us to stand firm on the truth of the cross and the grace found in Jesus.

So, today, choose to let go of your old identity and embrace your true identity in Jesus Christ. Begin to live boldly in the freedom God has granted to you. Give thanks to God for His eternal love and continuous work in your heart and your mind, and ask Him for mercy and the ability to let go of the past and embrace your true, God-given identity.

PRAYER

Heavenly Father, I praise You for the grace You have given to me and the truth You speak over my life. I worship You for the identity You have given to me in Jesus Christ and for the victory guaranteed by His blood that was shed for me on the cross. I praise You for Your Holy Spirit, who testifies to this truth within my heart. I am who You say I am, and I will follow You all the days of my life. Amen.

Letting Go of the Past

Dear brothers and sisters, I have not achieved it,
but I focus on this one thing: Forgetting the past
and looking forward to what lies ahead,
I press on to reach the end of the race and
receive the heavenly prize for which God,
through Christ Jesus, is calling us.

PHILIPPIANS 3:13–14 NLT

Letting go of the past can be difficult for many of us. It is easy to get trapped in feelings of shame, guilt, or regret, and to let our past mistakes define us. But as followers of Jesus Christ, we are called to something greater.

God has given us a new identity in Christ, one that is not defined by our past mistakes or failures. When we come to Jesus and confess our sins, He forgives us and makes us new. We are no longer prisoners of our past, but instead we are free to live in the present and look forward to the future.

It is important to remember that letting go of the past doesn't mean forgetting it entirely. Our past experiences, good or bad, have shaped us into the people we are today. But we can't let our past hold us back from becoming who God created us to be.

As we let go of the past, we can look forward to the prize that God has promised us in Christ Jesus. Our lives have meaning and purpose because we are called to run the race of faith and to reach the finish line, where Jesus is waiting for us. And as we run, we can trust in God's strength and mercy to guide us and sustain us.

So let us come before God with open and grateful hearts, confessing our sins and asking for His forgiveness and healing. Let us trust in the power of His grace to help us let go of the past and to run the race of faith with perseverance. And let us be confident that that future God has for us is one of hope, joy, and eternal life in Jesus Christ.

> **PRAYER**
>
> *Jesus, I adore You, for nothing is impossible with You. Your strength enables me to accomplish whatever goal You set before me. I praise You for Your Word, which empowers me to overcome any situation. Jesus, I thank You for Your comfort and encouragement in times of need. I give all glory and honor to You alone! Amen.*

SECTION: DEEP FORGIVENESS

God Commands Forgiveness

*"You must be compassionate, just as your
Father is compassionate.
Do not judge others, and you will not be judged.
Do not condemn others, or it will all come back against you.
Forgive others, and you will be forgiven."*

LUKE 6:36–37 NLT

Forgiveness is not just a suggestion; it is a commandment from God. It is not something that we should do if we feel like it or if we think the other person deserves it. We are called to forgive, to show mercy, and not to judge or condemn others. This can be a difficult concept to grasp—and an even more difficult concept to live out, especially when we have been hurt by someone else.

However, when we look at the example that God has set for us, we can see how important forgiveness is. God does not hold our own sins against us; He forgives us out of His compassion and love. We do not deserve to be forgiven, yet God offers us grace and mercy freely. It is because of this grace that we are able to forgive others who have hurt us.

Forgiveness is not something that we can do on our own. We need the help of the Holy Spirit to enable us to forgive as we have been forgiven. We must surrender our hearts to God and allow Him to minister to the areas where mercy does not yet reign. It is important that we reflect on the times when we have withheld forgiveness and allow the Holy Spirit to exchange our heart of stone for one of flesh.

We must also remember that forgiveness is not just a onetime event; it is a continual process of choosing to let go of the hurt and pain that others have caused us. It may take time to fully forgive someone, but with the help of the Holy Spirit, we can let go of the bitterness and resentment we may feel.

Forgiveness is a commandment, not a recommendation. We are called to forgive as we have been forgiven. It is not always an easy task, but with the help of the Holy Spirit, we can choose to show mercy and grace to others. Let us reflect on the love and compassion that God has shown to us and extend that same love to those around us. By choosing to forgive, we allow the love of Christ to transform our lives and the lives of those around us.

PRAYER

God, I praise You, for Your mercies are unending; they are renewed every single morning. I give You all the honor and glory, for there is none like You. You forgive my sins and restore my soul. I worship You, for there is no one gracious like You. I praise You, for Your faithfulness knows no end! Amen.

Limitless Forgiveness

Then Peter came to Jesus and asked,
"Lord, when my fellow believer sins against me,
how many times must I forgive him?
Should I forgive him as many as seven times?" Jesus answered,
"I tell you, you must forgive him more than seven times.
You must forgive him even if he wrongs you seventy times seven."

MATTHEW 18:21-22 NCV

Forgiveness is a divine directive that we are commanded to follow. It is not always an easy task, especially when we have been wronged multiple times. However, the only condition placed upon forgiveness is that it must be inexhaustible. We are to have mercy and to show grace repeatedly, no matter how many times we are wronged.

It is said that withholding forgiveness is like drinking poison and expecting another's death. It is completely pointless and fatal only to us. Holding on to offenses and nursing grudges will bring us nothing but evil. It will allow bitterness and hurt to grow roots within our souls, suffocate all manner of joy, and stifle any hope for a future. Therefore, we must forgive.

Sometimes pain and pride will tell us it is impossible to let go and forgive repeatedly. However, we know that God's love and grace are limitless. We need to think of all the times when God forgave us, no matter how grievous or heinous our sins were. We must confess our weakness to the Holy Spirit, sharing with Him our wounds and weariness and asking for His help to overcome the evil that was done against us.

We can ask God to fill us with His love, to give us the ability to have mercy and compassion as He does. He can remove our hurt and hatred and heal and restore us. We must guard our hearts from pride and presumption and ask the Holy Spirit to empower us to show grace toward the offenses of others.

As we forgive others, we become God's living example of grace in this world. We pour out His love and kindness to others, even when they do not seek our forgiveness. Forgiveness must be limitless, and we must choose to be God's living example of grace every day.

Thank God today for His kindness and patience toward you, for not keeping a record of your wrongdoings. Thank Him for all the times when He made you righteous and forgave your sins. Trust in the Holy Spirit's help to overcome the evil done against you and to forgive all those who have wronged you.

PRAYER

Lord, I praise You for Your faithfulness. I adore You, for Your love is unending and unmeasurable. I praise You, for You are gracious and kind, and Your forgiveness is vast and inexhaustible. I give You my adoration, for You have overcome all sin and conquered all hate. Righteousness and truth are found only in You. Amen.

Sow Forgiveness, Harvest Blessings

Plant the good seeds of righteousness,
and you will harvest a crop of love.
Plow up the hard ground of your hearts,
for now is the time to seek the Lord,
that He may come and shower righteousness upon you.

HOSEA 10:12 NLT

Forgiveness is not always easy, especially when we have been deeply hurt or wronged by someone. We may feel that by forgiving, we are accepting defeat and letting the other person off the hook. But the truth is, forgiveness is for our own benefit. It is a spiritual principle that activates God's legal spiritual authority to bless us, to be merciful and gracious to us.

The Law of the Harvest is a biblical principle that teaches us that our choices and actions dictate what we receive from God. When we choose to sow forgiveness and grace into the lives of those who have wronged us, we are ensuring our own victory. We are breaking up the hard ground in our lives and preparing for ourselves a harvest of justice and goodness.

God does not excuse evil behavior by reason of retaliation or provocation. He calls us to break the cycle of unforgiveness and seek to do what is good and just in His eyes. This means letting go of grudges, hatred, and bitterness, instead sowing forgiveness and grace wherever we go. It means seeking to cultivate a harvest of God's goodness and His faithful love, of His blessings and His divine favor.

We can only do this with the help of the Holy Spirit. We come before God and confess our sins to Him, asking for His aid in planting our harvest. We ask the Holy Spirit to transform our hearts and fill us with His grace and determination to sow forgiveness.

As we dwell on God's grace for us, we can thank Him for His love, which is greater than any hurt we may experience. We can thank the Holy Spirit for empowering us to overcome bitterness and for past experiences, in which God's grace transformed our hearts. We can ask God to fill us with His powerful love and to rain righteousness over our lives.

Choose today to break the cycle of unforgiveness and step into the amazing future God has for you. Sow forgiveness and grace, preparing for yourself a harvest of justice and goodness. Trust in God's love and faithfulness to see you through.

PRAYER

God, I give You praise, for Your justice is perfect. I worship You, for Your righteousness is true and will not be withheld from Your people. You pour out Your mercy on my life, and with Your lovingkindness, You have my heart. I praise You, for You are the everlasting God, and Your goodness and faithfulness know no end. Amen.

Love As Jesus Loved

Jesus said, "So now I am giving you a new commandment:
Love each other. Just as I have loved you,
you should love each other.
Your love for one another will prove
to the world that you are My disciples."

JOHN 13:34-35 NLT

As followers of Jesus, we are commanded to love others as God has loved us. This means giving the very best of ourselves, holding no grudges, and keeping no scores. We are to show mercy and grace, even in the face of betrayal.

Jesus demonstrated this love and forgiveness time and time again, but nowhere is this truth made clearer than at the scene of the Last Supper. Jesus was fully aware that Judas was about to betray Him, yet He still offered him a seat at the table. In full knowledge of what was to happen, Jesus still offered grace and mercy, because His actions did not depend on Judas.

We are called to love and to live as Christ did. The closest we will ever come to personifying Jesus this side of eternity is when we forgive someone who does not deserve nor want our forgiveness, because that is exactly what Jesus did for all of us. Consider God's unmatched love in our lives and thank Him for it. Thank Him for His love, which has no limits and affords us constant forgiveness for all our offenses. Take a moment to thank Jesus for not holding our wrongs against us and for giving us compassion in place of condemnation.

It is important to think about past experiences in which God's love gifted us with mercy. We should thank Him for all the past blessings of His grace in our lives and for those still to come.

God is present, and He is listening to you this day. Jesus died for you while you were still lost in your sins, still His enemy. He understands the challenge of this task He has set before you, the task of forgiveness. This becomes your opportunity to approach the throne of God and ask for His divine help.

We can ask God for His mercy to flood our souls, to fill us to overflowing, and to permeate every area of our hearts. As we ask the Holy Spirit to teach us to forgive all who wrong us, regardless of whether they are friend or foe, He promises to do so. If we allow Christ to rule in our hearts, His likeness will be seen in our actions. We must forgive others, be compassionate, and demonstrate mercy. We are called to love others as we have been loved by God.

Seize this day, this opportunity to demonstrate God's love to the world! Offer grace and sprinkle your actions with kindness; answer strife with peace; strive toward being a true witness of God's love and forgiveness to all.

PRAYER

Lord, I praise You for giving me the very best of who You are. You demonstrated Your love for me through Your actions at the cross. I exalt You, Lord, for Your love is unrestrained and unconditional. You withhold no good thing from me, and You love me completely. Help me to love others in this same way. Amen.

Overcoming Evil with Good

Do not let evil defeat you, but defeat evil by doing good.

ROMANS 12:21 NCV

As we journey through this life, we are bound to encounter evil in various forms. It could be in the hurtful words that are spoken to us, the betrayal of a trusted friend, or the unfair treatment we receive from others. Evil takes on many guises, but the most prevalent of them all is hurt and hate.

The problem with evil is that it feeds on negativity and discord. It thrives on anger, bitterness, and an unwillingness to forgive. If we are not careful, it can easily consume us, leaving us bitter, resentful, and filled with hatred. That is why it is so important to defeat evil, fighting against it at every turn.

The battle against evil is not an easy one. Human nature predisposes us to seek retribution for any offense committed against us. We want to get even, to make the other person pay for what they have done. But this mindset is self-destructive and goes against everything God teaches us to do.

We cannot defeat evil with evil. We are called to resist the urge to respond in kind when someone wrongs us. Instead, we stand firm in the truth of God's goodness and fight the real enemy. We overcome evil with good.

This battle against evil can be intense and brutal, both internally and externally. But we persevere in mercy and grace, knowing that victory is attainable. We can look to Jesus as our example, who opposed evil with goodness and poured out unrelenting mercy, unconditional grace, and forgiveness at the cross.

We have a choice in how we react to evil. We can either let it defeat us or overcome it with the goodness found in God's grace. God has called us to a victorious life filled with His love, grace, and goodness. And we can rest in the knowledge that His love gives us strength and with it, we can overcome any form of evil.

Today, choose to overcome evil with good. Stand your ground in the truth of God's goodness and fight the real enemy. Never forget the intensity and depth of your heavenly Father's love for you, which gives you the strength to overcome any evil that comes against your life.

PRAYER

Heavenly Father, when I look to the cross, I praise You, for Your love is great. I praise You for sending Your Son to sacrifice Himself for me. By Your goodness and the strength of Your power, You have redeemed me. You do not hide Yourself from me, and You give Your goodness without measure. I sing Your praises, for You overcame evil and defeated the grave. Your lovingkindness has restored my soul. Amen.

Kindness Overcomes Evil

If your enemies are hungry, give them food to eat.
If they are thirsty, give them water to drink.
You will heap burning coals of shame on their heads,
and the Lord will reward you.

PROVERBS 25:21-22 NLT

If you are a follower of Jesus Christ, you are called to live a life that reflects the love of God. This love is not just reserved for those who love us in return or for those who are easy to love. No, this love extends to those who cause us harm and those who are our enemies.

It can be difficult to extend love and kindness to those who have hurt us, but the Bible tells us that this is the very thing we should do. In fact, repaying evil with goodness is the only way to defeat evil. As followers of Christ, we have been given the Holy Spirit to enable us to love the way that Jesus did.

It is important to remember that when we show kindness to our enemies, we are not just being nice. We are actively defeating the power of evil within our lives. Kindness kills toxic environments, resentment, bitterness, anger, and hate. It's a powerful weapon that we have been given to combat the darkness in our world.

Jesus demonstrated this kind of love when He died on the cross for our sins. He chose to repay evil with goodness and grace, resulting in His victory over death and the restoration of all mankind. We, too, are called to extend this same kind of love to those around us.

We can't do any of this on our own. We need the help of the Holy Spirit to enable us to be compassionate and to show grace to those who don't deserve it. We need to be honest with God in prayer and ask Him to increase our mercy for others, making us more like Jesus.

Today, choose to repay evil with goodness. Be kind to those who hurt you and extend grace to those who don't deserve it. As you do this, you will see the very best of God's goodness in your life, and you will be a light in the darkness for all to see.

PRAYER

Jesus, thank You so much for loving me, for dying in my place when I was still Your enemy; for choosing to pour out Your grace and forgiveness over me; for sacrificing Yourself to restore my relationship with God, the Father. I worship You for Your love demonstrated in salvation. I praise You, for You alone are good. I worship Your name, for You are worthy of all the glory. Amen.

God's Justice and Forgiveness

Dear friends, never take revenge. Leave that to the righteous anger of God. For the Scriptures say, "I will take revenge; I will pay them back, says the Lord."

ROMANS 12:19 NLT

Vengeance belongs to God, but it can be challenging to accept this truth, especially when we feel wronged by others. However, we need to remember that God is the Supreme Judge, and only He can pass sentence and execute rightful punishment. It is not our responsibility to settle scores or attempt to right the wrongs done against us, and that can actually be a very freeing truth.

As you reflect on this, bring any feelings of frustration and helplessness to Jesus. Confess your owns sins to God and ask the Holy Spirit to transform your heart and mind and teach you how to forgive. Ask Him to remove all grudges and bitterness from your heart and give you the confidence to trust in the truth that God is fair and just.

It is essential to understand that our own human concept and understanding of justice may not align with God's. His justice is not merely about punishment, but it is also about righteousness, goodness, and the fulfillment of the dreams He has placed in our hearts.

Thank God for His justness and truth, that His Word is truth, and that His integrity cannot be swayed or corrupted. We can trust that He is the fair Judge who gives to each according to their deeds. We can have confidence in the truth that holy and righteous vindication cannot be thwarted.

We were not created to carry hatred or judge others. We were created for love, and we can choose freedom from the weight of revenge. Let us be filled with the confidence of Christ and His righteousness and trust that God will restore to us everything that we have lost.

Remember: vengeance belongs to God and God alone. We must trust Him and leave the execution of justice to Him. As we do this, we will experience freedom from bitterness and grudges, and we will be filled with the confidence of Christ and His righteousness.

PRAYER

O God Most High, there is no one like You. There is no one holy like You; there is no one beside You. Righteousness and justice are found only in Your hands. God, You judge the nations and give to each person according to what they have done. I will praise You as long as I live for Your righteousness and mercy that You have poured into my life. Amen.

SECTION:
NEW FRIENDSHIPS

Covenant Friendships

Jonathan made a solemn pact with David, because he loved him as he loved himself.

I SAMUEL 18:3 NLT

Friendship is a gift from God that is often taken for granted. We tend to think of friendship as a casual relationship that can be easily discarded when it becomes inconvenient or difficult. But true friendship is more than that. It is a covenant, a pact between two people that is rooted in love and mutual respect.

Throughout the Bible, we can see examples of covenants made between God and His people, and between people themselves. These covenants were not meant to be broken, and they were taken very seriously. When we enter into a friendship, we are making a similar commitment to another person.

The story of Jonathan and King David is a beautiful example of true friendship. Despite the fact that Jonathan was the son of King Saul, who was jealous of David and wanted to kill him, Jonathan recognized God's calling on David's life and chose to be his friend. Their friendship was not based on convenience or favorable circumstances; it was rooted in love and mutual respect.

As we reflect on the example of Jonathan and David, we see that true friendship requires effort and sacrifice. It means putting the needs of the other person before our own and being willing to forgive and work through difficult times. We must also remember that true friendship is a gift from God, and we should thank Him for the people in our lives who bless us with their friendship.

If you are struggling in your friendships, take a moment to present yourself before the Lord. Confess any sins that might be hindering your relationships and ask Him to place the right people in your life. Ask Him to bless you with the gift of friendship and to give you discernment over whom you should enter a covenant with.

Remember, friendship is a sacred commitment that should be taken seriously. But it is also a beautiful gift from God, one that brings joy and blessings into our lives. So let us cherish and honor the friendships that God has given us and choose to love others as we love ourselves.

PRAYER

Heavenly Father, I worship You and thank You for the abundant blessings You have poured into my life. I praise You for creating me with the capacity and the ability to experience friendship. Holy Spirit, I thank You for enabling and empowering me to love others as I love myself. Help me continue to be a good covenant-keeping friend. Amen.

The Blessing of Friendship

A friend loves you all the time,
and a brother helps in time of trouble.

PROVERBS 17:17 NCV

Friendship is a beautiful gift that God has given us. As humans, we are wired for connection and relationship, and friendship is one of the most important forms of connection we can have. However, in today's society, the term *friend* has been diluted and is used loosely to describe acquaintances and even strangers we meet on social media.

In the Bible, friendship is not something to be taken lightly. It is a covenant, a pledge to honor and cherish another person. The book of Proverbs says that a friend loves at all times, not just when it's convenient or beneficial for them. This means that true friendship is selfless and sacrificial. It seeks to give and serve rather than to gain.

Perhaps you are feeling lonely or isolated and have yet to experience the blessings of friendship. Or maybe you have been hurt by friends in the past and are hesitant to open yourself up to new relationships. Whatever your situation, know that God desires for you to have meaningful friendships in your life.

Take some time to reflect on the friendships in your life. Thank God for the people He has placed in your life, those who have been a constant source of love and support. And if you find yourself lacking in the friendship department, ask the Holy Spirit to help you cultivate healthy relationships. Ask Him to bring people into your life who will help you grow in your walk with God and who will also benefit from your friendship.

But being a good friend is not just about receiving love and support. It's also about giving it. Ask the Holy Spirit to teach you how to be a friend to others, how to love them through the good times and the bad. Be willing to put yourself out there and take a risk to build new friendships.

God designed us to live in community and to support one another. As you seek to be a friend to others, you will experience blessings in your own life. So, choose to love your friends through the ups and downs of life, and watch as you in turn are blessed by the constant blessing of friendship.

PRAYER

O God Most High, I praise You for Your Word, which is true and life-changing. I exalt You for Your grace and forgiveness, which Jesus poured out for me at Calvary, and for Your love, which enables me to live out my commitments. I worship You for helping me to understand the wisdom that is found in the Scriptures, and for empowering me to apply it daily to my life. Amen.

Steadfast Friends

One day while Jesus was teaching, some Pharisees and teachers of religious law were sitting nearby. (It seemed that these men showed up from every village in all Galilee and Judea, as well as from Jerusalem.) And the Lord's healing power was strongly with Jesus. Some men came carrying a paralyzed man on a sleeping mat. They tried to take him inside to Jesus, but they couldn't reach Him because of the crowd. So they went up to the roof and took off some tiles. Then they lowered the sick man on his mat down into the crowd, right in front of Jesus. Seeing their faith, Jesus said to the man, "Young man, your sins are forgiven."

LUKE 5:17–20 NLT

Friendship is steadfast. It is a bond between two individuals that is built on a foundation of love, trust, and commitment. It is a relationship that God desires for all of us to experience. The Bible teaches us that friendship is a blessing and that we should pursue it with all our hearts.

In John 15:13, Jesus says, "Greater love has no one than this: to lay down one's life for one's friends" (niv). This is the type of friendship that God desires for us. A friendship that is selfless and sacrificial, where we are willing to fight for our friends and to be there for them in their time of need.

The story above illustrates this truth in the best possible way. A group of men refused to give up and relentlessly pursued the blessing of a friend. They persevered in their task of finding a way to present their friend before the Lord, and because of their steadfast love and dedication, their friend was healed. This is the kind of friendship that changes lives.

God has called us to such friendship. He has called us to enter into a covenant of love with one another and to love each other at all times. He has called us to fight for each other's victories and to be a blessing unto others. He has called us to change lives and to experience the joy of giving and receiving steadfast love through friends.

If you are struggling with having friends or being a friend yourself, this is your opportunity to present your desires before the Lord. Confess your desires for deep friendship to God. Take a few minutes to dwell on God's goodness, to thank Jesus for the gift of steadfast friendship, and to ask Him to fill you with love and compassion for others.

Ask the Holy Spirit to give you steadfast friendships, to put people in your life who will cherish and love you, and who will fight for your victory beside you. Choose to love others as you love yourself, and watch as God's grace is displayed in your life.

Let us remember that friendship is steadfast. God wants us to experience friendship that perseveres in the face of need, a friendship that does not give up but rises to the occasion in the face of adversity. So let us choose this day to love others as we love ourselves, to be an instrument of blessing, and to experience the joy of giving and receiving steadfast love through our friends.

PRAYER

Lord, I praise You for Your Word, which is edifying and encouraging. I worship You for Your lovingkindness and Your grace. And I adore You for ministering this truth to my heart. In Your name, amen.

Practicing Empathy

Now Job had three friends: Eliphaz the Temanite, Bildad the Shuhite, and Zophar the Naamathite. When these friends heard about Job's troubles, they agreed to meet and visit him. They wanted to show their concern and to comfort him. They saw Job from far away, but he looked so different they almost didn't recognize him. They began to cry loudly and tore their robes and put dirt on their heads to show how sad they were. Then they sat on the ground with Job seven days and seven nights. No one said a word to him because they saw how much he was suffering.

JOB 2:11–13 NCV

The story of Job in the Bible is a powerful testimony of faith and friendship. Job, a righteous man, experienced extreme suffering and loss. Despite being blameless and upright, he was subjected to trials and tribulations that shook his faith to the core. Yet, in the midst of his pain and anguish, Job's friends stood by him, empathizing with his suffering and sharing in his sorrow.

Friendship, at its core, is empathetic. It is the ability to connect with someone on a deep level and to feel their pain and joy as if it were our own. This is precisely what Job's friends did. They did not offer simplistic solutions or platitudes. Instead, they sat with him, mourned with him, and showed him compassion.

In our own lives, we may struggle with empathy. It is easy to become self-absorbed and to focus solely on our own needs and desires. However, as followers of Christ, we are called to love one another and to bear each other's burdens. This means being willing to enter into the suffering of others and to offer comfort and support.

As we reflect on the example of Job's friends, let us ask God to give us hearts of compassion and empathy. Let us confess our sins and ask the Holy Spirit to work in us, enabling us to love others as ourselves. May we be grateful for the friendships God has given us and seek to be a blessing to those around us. Let us choose to embrace love and to share in bearing the burdens of our friends, trusting that God will use us to minister to others and bring glory to His name.

PRAYER

Heavenly Father, I praise You for Your vast greatness and Your infinite wisdom. For who is like You, God? By Your voice You created the heavens and set the foundations of the earth. Life and death are held in the very palm of Your hand. No one in heaven or earth can ever compare to You! Lord, give me an empathetic heart for those around me today. Amen.

Being Accountable

*Wounds from a sincere friend
are better than many kisses from an enemy.*

PROVERBS 27:6 NLT

As humans, we crave companionship and connection with others. We seek out people who can support us, laugh with us, and share in our joys and struggles. One of the most important aspects of any meaningful friendship is accountability. It may not always be pleasant, but it is a necessary component of growth and improvement.

It is easy to offer flattery and compliments to our friends, but it takes true love and courage to address uncomfortable truths. It is in these moments of vulnerability that we can truly show our love for our friends. We must be willing to step on their toes, to tell them when they are veering off course, or when their actions may have negative consequences. It is in these moments that we demonstrate our commitment to their well-being and our love for them.

Of course, accountability is not always easy. Some of us are naturally skilled at addressing difficult issues, while others may struggle with social anxiety and confrontation. However, as Christians, we are reminded that we are not alone in our efforts to love our friends well. God is always with us, and He will provide us with the strength and courage we need to be good friends.

As we reflect on our own friendships, we can take time to thank God for the friends who have spoken truth into our lives.

We remember the times when correction led to positive outcomes, and we thank God for His wisdom and guidance. We also pray for His help in being better friends to those around us, asking Him to teach us to love our friends as we love ourselves.

Ultimately, accountability is an essential part of any meaningful relationship. We must be willing to speak truth in love, and to embrace the truths spoken to us by our friends. We must trust in the wisdom of God and allow His love to flow through us into our friendships. May we all seek to be better friends, and to help each other grow and mature in our faith.

PRAYER

Lord God, I praise You for Your Word that does not return without doing the work You have sent it to do; it always fulfills its purpose! Jesus, You are a friend who sticks closer than a brother, and I thank You for all the lessons You continuously teach me as I follow Your lead in all my relationships. Amen.

Interceding for Your Friends

Jesus prayed, "I am praying for them [Jesus's disciples]. I am not praying for the world but for those whom you have given me, for they are yours.... And I am no longer in the world, but they are in the world, and I am coming to you. Holy Father, keep them in your name, which you have given me, that they may be one, even as we are one."

JOHN 17:9, 11 ESV

Friendship is a precious gift from God, one that involves prayer—praying for yourself and praying for your friends. Prayer is a powerful tool that allows us to communicate with God, and Jesus knew this well. He often prayed to God the Father for protection and unity between His disciples and between them and God.

As believers, we are called to follow Jesus's example of intercession and pray for our friends. Prayer is not simply wishful thinking or positive vibes but a petition before the Lord most High. We are invited to make our requests known to God, who promises to hear and answer us.

In seeking God's face and praying for our friends, we wage spiritual warfare on each other's behalf. We intentionally and specifically intercede for their spiritual and physical well-being, asking God to protect them and to strengthen their relationships with Him and with others.

Perhaps we have not been praying for our friends as we should. Maybe we have not been praying at all, and our prayer life is struggling. But the good news is that we can present ourselves before the Lord, confess our sins, and ask for His forgiveness and help.

As we pray, we can thank God for the favor He has shown us and for all the blessings He has bestowed upon us. We can thank Jesus for His blood that made a way for us to enter the Holy of Holies and for welcoming us into His secret place. We can thank the Holy Spirit for teaching us to pray as we should and for interceding on our behalf before God.

God is present and listening to us. We can approach His throne of mercy with boldness, asking the Holy Spirit to teach us to be intercessors and to love our friends as Jesus loved His disciples. We can be encouraged in knowing that God hears our prayers and that they matter to Him.

We should always remember that friendship calls for intercession. Let us follow Jesus's example and pray for our friends, asking God to protect them and to strengthen their relationship with Him and with others. May we approach God in prayer today with boldness, seeking His face and asking Him to teach us to be intercessors.

PRAYER

Dear heavenly Father, I worship You for who You are. Your wisdom brings joy and peace to my life. I adore You for Your patience is eternal and Your grace is immeasurable and inexhaustible. You alone are worthy of all my praise! Amen.

True Selflessness

"There is no greater love than to lay down one's life for one's friends."

JOHN 15:13 NLT

Friendship is an essential part of our lives, and it is a beautiful thing to have friends who love and care for us. However, the true essence of friendship is not about what we can gain, but about what we can give. Friendship is selfless, and there is no greater example of friendship than the cross.

Jesus Christ's sacrifice on the cross was the ultimate display of His love and friendship for us. He gave up His life so that we could have life, and His suffering was for our peace. He put our needs before His own, and His love for us was so great that He laid down His life for us.

Jesus's friendship was not self-serving, but rather, it was about serving others in love. He taught us that the standard of friendship is to put the needs of others before our own, just as He did for us. Jesus's love for us was selfless, and His empathy was unmatched. His Holy Spirit is always working to convict us of our sins and to minister the truth of friendship within our hearts.

If you are struggling to understand or accept this truth, you can approach God with boldness and ask Him to remove your heart of stone and give you a heart of flesh. You can ask the Holy Spirit to help you love others as you are loved by God. You can pray for a selfless love that gives without reservations or expectations.

Friendship should always be selfless, and Jesus Christ set the standard of what a true friend looks like. His sacrifice on the cross was the ultimate display of His love for us, and it should inspire us to love others with the same selflessness. Let us choose to live and love as Jesus did, to rise to the challenge of the standard set before us, and to be to others the friend Christ is to us.

> **PRAYER**
>
> *Lord, I praise You for Your selfless example of friendship, for dying on the cross so that I could spend eternity with You. I love You, and I thank You for Your constant work in my life.*

SECTION: MORE PRODUCTIVITY

Purposeful Creation

*God blessed them and said,
"Have many children and grow in number.
Fill the earth and be its master.
Rule over the fish in the sea and over the birds in the sky
and over every living thing that moves on the earth."*

GENESIS 1:28 NCV

Consider this amazing truth: you were created with a purpose! That purpose does not come from yourself or what you determine you want to do with your life. No, your purpose is not self-defined. It was given to you by your Creator, who formed you with a plan in mind.

In a world that constantly bombards us with messages of self-discovery and self-fulfillment, it can be easy to forget that our true purpose lies in our relationship with God. It is through this relationship that we find our true identity and our real purpose in life.

God created us to be productive, to work alongside Him in the ongoing work of creation. This does not mean that we are called to be workaholics or to find our worth in our accomplishments, but rather that we are called to be faithful stewards of the gifts and talents that God has given us.

When we embrace this truth and seek God's will for our lives, we can experience a sense of fulfillment and purpose that goes beyond anything that the world can offer. We can trust that God has good plans for our lives, and that He will equip us to fulfill them.

So today, let us take a moment to thank God for our lives and our purpose. Let us seek His guidance and direction for our lives and ask Him to reveal His plans for us. And let us commit to living out His purpose for our lives, to be productive and faithful stewards of all that He has given us.

Greet this day in God's strength, confident in His purpose for your life, and may everything you do today bring glory and honor to Him!

PRAYER

God, I praise You for Your power and love, which is demonstrated throughout Your creation. All Your work You do in faithfulness. I worship You for creating me with a plan and for a purpose. I exalt You, Lord, for the wonderful things to come! I praise You for the good work You have conceived and prepared for my life. Amen.

Committing to God's Blessing

Put GOD in charge of your work, then what you've planned will take place.

PROVERBS 16:3 THE MESSAGE

Commitment to God is a fundamental principle in the life of a believer. It requires constant work, and it is not always easy to uphold your loyalty and devotion regardless of unforeseen circumstances, unpleasant situations, or human temptations. However, committing to God means you pledge yourself to Him, making the conscious choice to dedicate everything you do to Him. When you make this commitment, you will experience success and achieve productivity.

The Bible teaches that success comes from committing your projects unto God. To commit something to God means to dedicate it to Him, to center and focus it on Him. When your plans are centered and focused on God, your actions will align with God's commandments, and you will have God's blessing. This is why it is essential to remember to put God first in everything you do.

Sometimes we may forget this and choose to leave God out of our plans. We may be overtaken by rebellious thoughts, and our sinful desires may prevent us from even thinking of God. However, regardless of your current state, you have an opportunity in this moment to turn to Christ and ask the Holy Spirit to help you remove anything keeping you from committing to God.

Take a few minutes right now to dwell on the blessings of God.

Thank the Lord for His unending mercies and benevolent grace. Thank God for His instructions and His guidance. Thank Him for sending His Holy Spirit to help you succeed in your endeavors. Thank the Holy Spirit for enabling you to understand God's Word and apply it to your life. Thank Him for teaching you, for helping you dedicate your goals and projects to God.

God is present right now, and He is listening to you. God longs to bless you and make your plans succeed. He knows the difficulties and challenges you face in this life. As His child, you have access to His throne room. So come before Him and ask Him for aid. Ask the Holy Spirit to imprint God's words upon your heart, to enable you to live out the commandments found in Scripture. Ask the Holy Spirit to help you commit all you do unto Him and bless your plans.

As you commit your activities to the Lord, you will experience peace. Dedicate what you wish to accomplish to God, and you will be productive. Choose this day to entrust your plans to God, to depend on Him, and to do all things for Him and through Him. Open yourself to the blessings God has prepared for you.

PRAYER

Lord Jesus, I bless Your name. I praise You, for You are the everlasting God. You do not faint or grow weary; Your love and kindness toward me will never cease. God, I praise You, for You are mighty. You are able to do above and beyond anything I could ever imagine. Thank You for filling me with divine strength and for establishing the works of my hands. Amen.

Focusing on God

In all the work you are doing, work the best you can. Work as if you were doing it for the Lord, not for people. Remember that you will receive your reward from the Lord, which He promised to His people. You are serving the Lord Christ.

COLOSSIANS 3:23–24 NCV

As we navigate through life, we encounter many distractions that pull us away from our focus on God. We often find ourselves caught up in the daily routines of life and forget the purpose for which we were created. However, we must always remember that our focus will shape who we are and what we do. Therefore, it is important to understand God's plan and purpose for our lives.

When we recognize that we were created by God, God becomes our focal point. We operate from a mentality that Jesus is our incentive, and He is alongside us as we work to achieve our plans. With God as our focus, we do everything as if doing it unto Him. Our thoughts and actions become centered on Christ, and we become proactive rather than reactive.

The opinions of others no longer dictate our behavior, and we no longer work to please or impress those around us. Instead, everything we do is done to bring glory to God. As we commit our plans to God and focus on Him, He blesses the work of our hands, and we become productive.

To stay focused on God, we must present ourselves before the Lord and confess our sins. We thank God for His care, presence, mercy, blessings, goodness, grace, and the work of the Holy

Spirit within us. We lift our voice in prayer to God and ask for His heavenly help, wisdom, discernment, dedication, and strength to persevere in all our goals.

As we serve Christ, we work as if we are working for the Lord and not for people, for our reward comes from God. We chase after the fullness of what God has for us, knowing that we are more than conquerors in Jesus Christ.

Make God your focal point and commit your plans to Him. Then work diligently, as if you were working for the Lord, and remain focused on Him, knowing that your reward comes from Him. With God as your focus, you can accomplish great things and become all that He created you to be.

PRAYER

Lord God, I praise You, for You are great and mighty, and there is nothing hidden from Your sight. You see all things, and You give to each person according to their works. I worship You, Lord, for You are fair and just. You will not allow the righteous to be shaken. I worship You, for strength and grace come from You alone. I bless Your name—all glory, honor, and power are Yours! Amen.

Consider the Ant

Take a lesson from the ants, you lazybones.
Learn from their ways and become wise!
Though they have no prince or governor or ruler to make them work,
they labor hard all summer, gathering food for the winter.

PROVERBS 6:6–8 NLT

Diligence and personal accountability are two critical values that can help us live a productive and meaningful life. The example of ants, as shared in the above proverb, teaches us that no matter how small or insignificant we may feel, we have the potential to accomplish great things if we are diligent and work together.

King Solomon, the author of Proverbs, warns against laziness and calls us to personal accountability. He encourages us to be like the ants who work diligently at their own task, without requiring supervision or constant commands. We should not wait to be told what needs to be done, nor make excuses for laziness. Instead, we must hold ourselves accountable to the goals and tasks set before us and strive to be diligent and responsible in completing them.

As believers, we have access to the Holy Spirit, who can empower us to apply work ethics and work hard. We can come before God, confess our sins, and ask for His help in applying ourselves to our endeavors. We can thank Him for the blessing of wisdom found throughout Scripture and for providing correction that will produce a better future and a better life.

Today, choose to apply God's wisdom to your life and be responsible in your tasks. May you seek to diligently complete your work, hold yourself accountable to what is right, and do what must be done at the proper time. As you do this, you can trust that God will bless the works of your hands and increase your productivity.

PRAYER

Lord God, I thank You for Your infinite wisdom. I adore You for the knowledge and the understanding that I find in Your holy Word. Holy Spirit, I invite You into my life and praise You for enabling me to receive and apply Your wisdom into my life. Amen.

Using Time Wisely

Be very careful how you live.
Do not live like those who are not wise, but live wisely.
Use every chance you have for doing good,
because these are evil times.
So do not be foolish but learn
what the Lord wants you to do.

EPHESIANS 5:15–17 NCV

Time is a gift that God has given to us all. We each have a limited amount of it, and it is up to us to use it wisely. We cannot control time, but we can control how we use it. We must be careful not to let procrastination steal our time away from us.

God has called us to be productive and to use our time wisely. We can use our time to accomplish His will and to be a blessing to those around us. This means that we must be diligent in our tasks and make the most of every opportunity that comes our way.

As we spend time with God, reading His Word and seeking His will, we will gain wisdom and insight into how we should use our time. We will learn to prioritize our tasks and to focus on the things that are most important. We will also learn to avoid the things that are superficial and superfluous.

When we use our time wisely, we will see the fruits of our labor. We will be able to accomplish more and to be more effective in our work. We will also be able to more fully enjoy the blessings that God has for us.

Let us thank God for the wisdom that He has imparted to us through His Word. Let us thank Him for His mercy and grace that enable us to be productive and to accomplish His will. Let us also ask the Holy Spirit to guide us and to help us use our time in a smart and efficient way.

As you dedicate your plans to God and focus on Him, you will see your productivity bloom. You will be able to make the most of every opportunity that comes your way, and you will be a blessing to those around you. So choose to use your time wisely and trust in Jesus Christ to guide you and lead you in all you do.

PRAYER

God, I worship You for You have not given me a spirit of fear, but of power and of love and of a sound mind. I praise You for granting me Your unmatched grace, Your grace that provides my true identity, found in You. I worship You for Your lovingkindness shown throughout my life. You are always with me—You never leave me nor forsake me. I praise Your holy name for victory and power belong to You alone. Amen.

Carpe Diem!

*Whatever your hand finds to do, do it with all your might,
for in the realm of the dead, where you are going,
there is neither working nor planning nor knowledge nor wisdom.*

ECCLESIASTES 9:10 NIV

Carpe diem: Seize the day! This famous Latin phrase urges us to make the most of our lives while we still have the chance. The truth is that we all share the same fate—death. No one is guaranteed the time they will have here on earth. This means that every moment we are given is precious and should not be wasted.

God wants us to live our lives to the fullest and not be idle. We must be productive and use our time wisely. We were created for a purpose, and we should strive to fulfill that purpose every day. We can work to be grateful for the blessings we have received and for the ones still to come. We cannot be discouraged by the challenges we face, but instead, we should present ourselves before the Lord and confess our sins to Him.

In whatever season we find ourselves, there is always a reason to be thankful. Take a moment to set aside your concerns and acknowledge your blessings. Thank God for His plans and His purpose for your life. Thank Him for His wisdom and the blessing it brings. Thank Him for teaching us to value and redeem our time.

We must be mindful of our mortality and ask the Holy Spirit to convict us of the need for urgency. We can then dedicate our plans unto God and focus on Him. We can ask Him to fill us with determination and discipline to complete our tasks. We can ask

Him to give us wisdom in managing our time and behavior. We can ask Him to bless the work of our hands and help us increase our productivity.

At the end of our lives, we will be judged not by the number of possessions we had, but by the impact we made on the world. We should not carry regret with us into eternity. We must seize the opportunity God is giving us and give Him our all. We choose to live our lives for Christ.

Remember to *carpe diem* today! Seize the day! Make the most of the time you have been given and live your life to the fullest. Dedicate your plans to God and allow Him to bless all that you do. May you be productive and fulfill the purpose for which you were created, and may you be grateful for your blessings and thank God for His plans and purpose for your life.

PRAYER

Heavenly Father, I praise You for Your immeasurable wisdom and Your mighty strength. You give power to the weak, and for those who have no might, You increase strength. God, I thank You for enabling me to focus and to complete the task before me. I bless Your name, for You are great and greatly to be praised! Amen.

Productivity Brings Joy

You will enjoy what you work for,
and you will be blessed with good things.

PSALM 128:2 NCV

Productivity brings joy. As we strive to achieve our goals, we experience a sense of accomplishment that fills our hearts with joy. This joy is not just a result of our hard work but is a gift from God, who wired our brains to reward us for our necessary actions. He created us to be productive and to experience the joy found in the fruition of our efforts and hard work.

The human body is a wondrous display of God's power and greatness, but no other part of the body functions quite like the brain does. The brain controls the actions of the body, and its decision-making process is influenced by necessity and reward. Our brains reward us with chemicals that make us feel good when we accomplish imperative tasks. This reward system is a motivational tool that God uses to help us be more productive in life and to help us persevere in following through with our goals and responsibilities.

God wants us to be diligent and to work hard. We are not meant to be idle. We are meant to hold ourselves accountable, to dedicate our plans to Him, and to watch Him make those plans succeed. When we focus on Him, we receive the reward He has prepared for us.

Maybe you are struggling with persevering in your tasks, and you feel like you're being robbed of the joy of your labor. This is your opportunity to present yourself before God, confess your sins to Him, and ask for His strength and confidence.

God is here right now, and He is listening to you. Take a moment to thank Him for His goodness in your life, for providing you with the tools necessary for success, for His divine word that teaches, motivates, and encourages you, and for His favor over you in every project you set your hands to do.

As you set forth on your goals and projects, know that you are not alone. God longs to prosper your work and to see you enjoy your accomplishments. So choose this day to dedicate your endeavors to God and to persevere, so you may enjoy the rewards of your effort and hard work. May the Holy Spirit fill you with divine dedication and determination toward your tasks and empower you to see your work through to the fruition of your labor, so that you may live out God's goodness here on earth.

PRAYER

Jesus, I thank You for Your Word, which teaches me and guides me to greater things. I praise Your name, Lord, for Your wisdom grants blessings to those who obey You. Thank You for sending Your Holy Spirit, who empowers me to achieve the goals set before me. I worship You, O Lord, for I know I will see Your goodness here, in the land of the living. Amen.

SECTION:
REST AND RECOVER

Entering God's Rest

Jesus said, "Come to Me, all of you
who are tired and have heavy loads,
and I will give you rest.
Accept My teachings and learn from Me,
because I am gentle and humble in spirit,
and you will find rest for your lives.
The burden that I ask you to accept is easy;
the load I give you to carry is light."

MATTHEW 11:28–30 NCV

Life can be challenging and overwhelming, and at times we may feel exhausted and drained. But God wants to give us rest. He knows our struggles and challenges, and He longs to provide us with the rest we need to persevere. As we face hardships and pain in this fallen world, it is important that we stand our ground and fight. And amidst the hard times, we must also take time to rest and recover.

Jesus came to offer us salvation and to restore our weary souls. He wants to recover what the enemy has taken from us and to give us a sense of purpose and identity. When we choose to live under God's love and righteousness, we can experience His rest and find the strength we need to continue the fight.

As we thank God for His rest and grace, we come before Him and ask for His help. We ask Jesus to remove the burden of sin from our lives and to reveal His calling and work to us. We ask the Holy Spirit for an encounter with God's gentleness and for Him to refresh our weary souls.

God is present in this place, and He is listening to you. He wants you to give up the impossible task of carrying your own sins. He wants to impart His eternal kingdom to you and give you the rest you need to persevere. So choose to trust in God today and accept the rest and blessings He longs to give to you!

PRAYER

I praise You, Lord, for You are the mighty God, yet You see me and You love me. I worship You, Jesus, for Your grace poured out at Calvary, Your grace that covers my sins and restores my soul. Holy Spirit, I thank You for ministering to my soul today and for manifesting God's goodness in my life. Amen.

God's Presence Brings Rest

The LORD replied,
"My Presence will go with you,
and I will give you rest."

EXODUS 33:14 NIV

God's presence brings rest. It is a promise that we can hold on to no matter how dark our situation may seem. We can find rest in God's presence because when God shows up, the atmosphere changes. There is an abundance of joy, chains are broken, captives are set free, and restoration and redemption are found.

We live in a world that can sometimes feel dark. When we follow the ways of the world, instead of the ways of God, it is almost impossible to find true and lasting rest.

Take a moment to reflect on the ways in which you need rest and refreshment. If you feel that God is far away, stop and think of what is preventing you from connecting with Him. Confess your sins to the Holy Spirit and share your weariness and weaknesses with Him.

Thank God for His Holy Spirit, who walks beside you. Thank Him for the peace and rest His presence brings. Thank the Lord for His kindness and goodness toward you. Thank Jesus for the blessing of eternal fellowship and for the access to God the Father that He grants you. Thank Him that His love will never change, that He will never withhold it from you.

Never forget that God is present with you in this moment, and He is listening to you. Come before Him and ask Him to reveal Himself to you. Ask God to fill you with His presence and pour out His Holy Spirit upon you. Ask Jesus to remove all obstacles standing in the way of your fellowship with Him. Ask Him to remove your heart of stone and give you a heart of flesh. Ask the Holy Spirit to alleviate and remove all weariness and fatigue. Ask Him to revive and restore every area of your life. Ask the Holy Spirit to minister God's goodness to your mind, body, and soul.

God's presence provides rest. Do not fear rejection and do not hesitate to approach God. Jesus has already pledged His unending love to you through His sacrifice on the cross. He promised to be with you until the end of the ages. Know that God wants you to experience His goodness here, in the land of the living. Reach out to Him today. Invite His holy presence to dwell within your heart and receive His rest today.

PRAYER

God, I praise You for Your unconditional love. I worship You for Your presence, which changes atmospheres. I exalt You, Lord, for You alone provide rest and recovery. I thank You that You are a wonder-working God. Holy Spirit, I adore You for Your gentle kindness, which ministers to my soul and spirit this day. Amen.

Gratitude Brings Rest

Enter His gates with thanksgiving;
go into His courts with praise.
Give thanks to Him and praise His name.

PSALM 100:4 NLT

Gratitude is a powerful tool in our spiritual journey. It opens doors to heavenly blessings and grants us access to God's presence, which brings us rest and renewal. When we are tired and weary, we must seek God, for only in His presence can we find the strength to persevere. We must not allow the devil to deceive us into thinking that we are forgotten or that God no longer cares. The blood of Jesus Christ has granted us access to the throne of grace, and we can approach God with confidence.

By acknowledging His goodness in our lives and thanking Him for it, we break through all lies we believe and go straight to God. Gratitude is like an arrow that pierces through all resistance that keeps us from the Lord. It unlocks access to heavenly blessings and invites God's presence to change our circumstances.

If we find ourselves struggling with gratitude, we can reach out to God and confess our sins to Him. We can take time to dwell on His grace, thank Him for His eternal love, and thank Jesus Christ for His sacrifice on the cross. We can also thank the Holy Spirit for ministering God's rest and renewal over us continuously.

As we praise God for everything He has done, is doing, and will do, we invite His presence into our lives. Where His presence is, there is fullness of joy and recovery. Gratitude is the reciprocal of grace, and when we choose to give God honor and glory, we position ourselves to receive more of His blessings.

Let us choose to be thankful in all circumstances, for this is God's will for us. Let us not focus on what we lack but fix our eyes on God's grace and be grateful. By doing so, we enter His gates with thanksgiving and His courts with praise, and we find rest and renewal in His presence.

PRAYER

Lord, I give You praise, for You are God over all. Compared to You, what is humanity, that You should be mindful of us? And still, in Your lovingkindness, You care for us and draw near to hear our cries. I worship You because Your love is pure and passionate, and You are a patient and personable God. There is none like You! Amen.

Restoration from the Lord

He energizes those who get tired, gives fresh strength to dropouts. For even young people tire and drop out, young folk in their prime stumble and fall. But those who wait upon God get fresh strength. They spread their wings and soar like eagles, they run and don't get tired, they walk and don't lag behind.

ISAIAH 40:30–31 THE MESSAGE

Life can be hard and unpredictable. No one is exempt from the challenges that come our way. However, God offers us restorative rest. When we trust in Him, we can experience His restorative power in our lives.

It's easy to rely on our own strength and capabilities. We live in a world that praises self-sufficiency and independence. However, our human strength is limited. We are prone to error and susceptible to failure. Eventually, we all get worn out. But God is infinitely mighty. He has immeasurable power and can restore our strength, mentally, spiritually, and physically.

When we come before God and seek His rest, we confess our sins and our weariness to Him. We need to acknowledge that we can't do this on our own. We need His help to overcome the challenges we face.

We can thank God for His everlasting and unfathomable loving kindness. We can thank Jesus for paying the price of our rest and renewal at the cross. We can thank the Holy Spirit for imparting

God's strength into our lives. When we seek God's restorative power, we can experience true transformation.

The Lord longs to give us rest and to restore our strength. We don't have to go through life tired and depleted. Jesus loves us and wants to renew our hearts and souls today. We can accept His gift of rest and recovery and allow Him to change our lives.

Come before God today and seek His restorative rest. Trust in Him and don't depend on yourself; depend only on Him. May God renew your heart and soul and give you the strength to persevere through any challenges you may face. May you experience the transformative power of God in your life and give Him all the praise and glory.

PRAYER

Heavenly Father, I praise You, for You are my Savior and my God. For Your name's sake, You deliver me and forgive my sins. I praise You, Jesus, for Your grace and Your goodness are given without measure. Holy Spirit, I thank You for refreshing my soul and renewing my mind. Amen.

Serving Others

"I will tell you the kind of fast I want: Free the people you have put in prison unfairly and undo their chains. Free those to whom you are unfair and stop their hard labor. Share your food with the hungry and bring poor, homeless people into your own homes. When you see someone who has no clothes, give him yours, and don't refuse to help your own relatives. Then your light will shine like the dawn, and your wounds will quickly heal. Your God will walk before you, and the glory of the Lord will protect you from behind."

ISAIAH 58:6–8 NCV

The prophet Isaiah reminds us that serving others brings restoration. It is not just about saying kind words, but it is about actively doing something for others. It is about loving our neighbors as we love ourselves. When we do this, we experience God's healing and restorative power.

We are called to be kind and compassionate to others. When we see someone in need, we should do something about it. Our actions should reflect the love of God. We do not have to do grand gestures to impress God or to show great love. When we do something that brings rest and restoration to others, God moves on our behalf and heals our own wounds.

We can examine our hearts and confess our sins and lack of love toward our neighbors to God. We then thank God for His restorative power, His life-giving word, and the Holy Spirit that enables us to love others.

God's instructions are clear: we are to seek justice, have compassion on the poor, feed the hungry, and share our resources with those who are less fortunate. When we do this, our light will shine like the break of day, and our wounds will heal. God's grace and glory will surround our lives.

Today, seize every opportunity you are given to be a blessing and to be blessed. Reach out to God and allow His light to shine through you and in you to everyone you meet. May you have a heart after His own so that you may love others as you have been loved. May you be a blessing today to those around you, and in doing so, you yourself will be blessed and restored.

PRAYER

Lord, I praise You for the promise of recovery. I worship You for Your Word, which gives me hope for the future, that brings blessings into my life and into the lives of those around me. Thank You for Your goodness in my life. Amen.

Provision through Prayer

After Job had prayed for his three friends,
the Lord made Job twice as rich as he had been before.

JOB 42:10 CEV

The story of Job in the Bible is a powerful testament to the strength of faith and the restorative power of prayer. Job suffered immense loss and pain, with no understanding of why God allowed such hardships to come upon him. Despite this, he refused to turn away from God, choosing instead to remain faithful even in the midst of his suffering.

In our own lives, we may face similar trials and tribulations that leave us feeling lost, alone, and without answers. But just as Job turned to prayer in his time of need, we too can find comfort and strength through prayer.

Through prayer, we can confess our sins and lift up those around us in need of God's grace and mercy. We can ask the Holy Spirit to help us remain faithful to God even when we don't understand our circumstances, and to teach us to have mercy and compassion for others.

It is important to remember that prayer has the power to restore and renew. Job saw this restoration firsthand in his life. Similarly, as we pray for others, God can pour out His restoration upon our own lives.

Let us choose to be vessels of blessing, allowing God to work through us to help others and to bring about His restoration in our own lives. Let us give thanks for all the blessings God has bestowed upon us and continue to seek His guidance and strength through prayer.

> **PRAYER**
>
> *Lord, I praise You for Your provision in my life. You are the God over all things, and You know Your creation like no other. In Your infinite mercies, You minister to me. Thank You for Your continual work in my life—today and every day. Amen.*

The Lord Refreshes My Soul

He refreshes my soul.
He guides me along the right paths for His name's sake.

PSALM 23:3 NIV

Life can often feel like a race, a never-ending marathon with no finish line in sight. We run and run, striving to achieve our goals and make something of ourselves, but often find ourselves faltering along the way. We grow weary and exhausted, our bodies and souls tired from the endless pursuit of success and happiness.

In these moments of weakness, it can be easy to lose faith in ourselves and in God. We question our abilities and wonder if we will ever make it to the finish line. But it is in these moments that we must turn to God, for it is through Him that we find rest and restoration.

God's rest brings restoration and righteousness. When we are tired and weary, God offers us a place of rest and renewal. He sees us in our struggles and knows exactly what we need before we even ask. All we have to do is trust in Him and allow Him to minister to our souls.

When we surrender ourselves to God, He not only restores our strength but also leads us on the path that leads to righteousness. He shows us the way to live a life worth living, a life filled with godly thoughts and actions, justice, and goodness. He gives us the strength to overcome our struggles and the grace to live out our dreams.

So, when you find yourself running on empty and ready to give up, remember that God is beside you. He will never let you down, not even one time. Take this opportunity to turn to Him, confess your sins, and ask for His grace. Thank Him for His goodness and mercy and allow Him to minister to your soul.

Thank God, for He restores your soul and establishes His righteousness in your life. Trust in Him and surrender to Him, and He will give you rest and show you how to live life to its fullest.

PRAYER

I praise You, Lord, for You are the living God. You have made me, and I am Yours. I will give thanks and bless Your name today, Jesus, for You are my Shepherd. You restore my soul and lead me into a righteous life. Thank You for Your constant loving guidance. Amen.

SECTION:
POSITIVE MINDSET

Godly Positivity

If our minds are ruled by our desires, we will die. But if our minds are ruled by the Spirit, we will have life and peace.

ROMANS 8:6 CEV

As we go through life, we encounter different situations and circumstances that shape our mindset. The experiences we have, the people we interact with, and the things we focus our thoughts on can either build us up or tear us down. However, as believers in Christ, we are called to have a godly mindset, one that is rooted in His truth and guided by His Spirit.

It is important to understand that our thoughts are not harmless, but rather powerful. They can either lead us toward life or toward death. We have a choice in which influence we allow to take root in our hearts.

God has given us the power to choose which mindset we allow to dictate our thoughts. We have the power to manifest what we ruminate on in our lives through our actions. If we dwell on the pleasures and desires of the flesh, our acts will follow suit. But if we focus on holy things and godly desires, our actions will produce good fruit.

It is so easy to get caught up in the things of this world and to be controlled by our sinful selves. But as we confess our sins to God and ask Him to minister to our minds, bodies, and souls, we can be transformed by His Spirit. We can ask the Holy Spirit to renew our minds as we read His Word, to overwhelm us with His presence, and to lead us toward a godly mindset.

Start the day by thanking God for His Holy Spirit. It is through Him that we are granted the power to change our mentality. Ask for His guidance in choosing life and peace over death and destruction. And always remember that God is present and listening to you, ready to transform you through the renewing of your mind. May you continually seek after a godly mindset and trust in His power to lead you toward His truth and His will for your life.

PRAYER

God, I praise You because Your Word is life, and Your Spirit gives peace. I adore You because You are good, You are kind, and Your mercies endure forever. I praise You for Your endless grace. You are so great—there is no one like You! Amen.

Choose a Godly Mindset

Think about the things of heaven, not the things of earth.

COLOSSIANS 3:2 NLT

To cultivate a godly mindset is a choice we must make daily. As individuals, God has given us the power to choose and decide for ourselves, and the first step toward obtaining a godly mindset is to choose Christ. When we choose Christ, our aim becomes heaven and not the things on this earth. Our focus should be on God and not on the worries and preoccupations of this world.

To maintain a heavenly mindset, we must continuously strive to stay in tune with the Spirit. God wants to speak to us concerning our mental state throughout the day. We need to let go of our old sinful ways and focus on Christ. This is a wonderful opportunity to present ourselves before the Lord, confess our sins, and ask Him to forgive and cleanse us.

Take a few minutes to dwell on the goodness of God and thank Him for His faithfulness. Also thank the Holy Spirit for renewing your mind through God's Word and for ministering God's truth into your heart. Ask the Holy Spirit to help you cultivate a godly mindset and remove your earthly mentality. Allow Him to put the desire within your heart for the things of heaven and focus on Christ.

Those who belong to Christ are to think of the things in heaven, not the things on earth. We choose to set our minds on godly things and cultivate a spiritual mindset in Christ. We invite the Holy Spirit to permeate our minds and be present in all we do and everywhere we go.

Having a godly mindset is a choice that you must make daily. You must choose Jesus, focus on Him, and strive to maintain a heavenly mindset. Choose to set your mind on godly things each day and invite the Holy Spirit to permeate your mind. Then you will see God change your mindset from negativity to positivity—from death to life.

> **PRAYER**
>
> *God, I praise You, for You are the beginning and the end of all things. God, I worship You, for You are the Alpha and the Omega, the first and the last. God, I thank You for being the Author and the Finisher of my faith. Amen.*

Fill Your Mind with the Word

Such things were written in the Scriptures long ago to teach us. And the Scriptures give us hope and encouragement as we wait patiently for God's promises to be fulfilled.

ROMANS 15:4 NLT

In a world full of negativity, it can be easy to lose sight of what is truly important in life. It is crucial that we maintain a positive mindset to overcome the challenges we face on a daily basis. But how can we achieve this when we are bombarded with negativity from every direction?

The answer is simple: turn to the Bible. To acquire a godly mindset, we must first get to know God Himself. And the best way to get to know God is through reading His Word. The Bible is God's divine gift to us, a tool for both instruction and blessing. When we read God's Word, our minds are renewed, our hearts are ministered to, and our souls are restored.

The Bible teaches us how to hope through patience and encouragement. It transforms our thoughts and gives us a heaven-focused mentality. It teaches us how to crucify our flesh, to walk in obedience and relationship with our heavenly Father, so that we can persevere and overcome in this world.

However, the Bible will do us no good if we do not read it. We must plug into God to receive His power. We cannot receive from God without His Word. So if we have been struggling to spend time reading our Bible, now is the time to change our situation.

We can present ourselves before the Lord, confess our sins, and ask Him for His forgiveness and His grace. We thank God for the blessing of the Scriptures, for His living and edifying Word, which is truth and unchanging. We ask the Holy Spirit to help us process God's Word, to give us revelation and understanding, and to enable us to acquire and maintain a godly mindset.

As you spend time with God and His Word, you will see His power radically transform your mindset. You will be able to maintain a positive and productive outlook on life, no matter what challenges come your way. So choose God today—and every day to come—and plug into His power through His Word.

PRAYER

Lord, I praise You for Your infinite knowledge and Your immeasurable wisdom. I praise You for the mind-changing power provided in Your Word, and I thank You that through Christ, who strengthens me, I can do all things. Amen.

Assurance in God

"For I know the plans I have for you," says the LORD.
"They are plans for good and not for disaster,
to give you a future and a hope."

JEREMIAH 29:11 NLT

Assurance in God is something that can bring great positivity and peace of mind to our lives. There is a sense of security that comes from knowing that our future is secure and that we are provided for. This assurance is a gift from God, and it's available to all who seek Him.

As we focus on cultivating a godly mentality and continuously read our Bible, we begin to receive assurance from God's Word. It ministers to our souls and transforms our minds, giving us a new outlook on life. It teaches us, guides us, and gives us confidence.

The more we trust in the Holy Spirit, the more confident we become in God's assurance. And as our relationship with God grows, His blessings begin to manifest in our lives, reinforcing our positivity and faith.

Perhaps you are feeling overwhelmed by fear and negativity. Maybe your confidence is not firmly placed in God. This is your chance to change your situation. Confess your sins to Jesus and ask Him for His forgiveness and assurance.

God's love for you will never fail, and His plans for you are good. Take a moment to remember past experiences of His goodness and thank Him for those memories. Then reach out boldly to God in the knowledge of His love and His promises.

Choose to step out in the assurance and confidence that the Holy Spirit gives. Embrace the positivity and peace of mind that come from knowing God's plans for you are good. And trust that He will continue to bless you as you seek the Lord and grow in your relationship with Him.

> **PRAYER**
>
> *Lord, I worship You for who You are. I praise You for Your infinite and unfailing love toward me. I know Your plans for me are better than anything I could ever imagine. I'm so grateful for what You are doing in my life! Amen.*

God Is Enough

The L{\sc ord} is my shepherd; I have everything I need.
He lets me rest in green pastures. He leads me to calm water.

PSALM 23:1–2 NCV

God is enough. This simple statement holds a profound truth that we often forget in our day-to-day lives. We get so caught up in the hustle and bustle of our daily routines that we forget to acknowledge the One who makes it all possible. We tend to have faith in God's assurance only when we feel secure in ourselves. But what happens when things go wrong? What happens when we lose our jobs, when we face financial difficulties, or when we encounter sickness and death? It is in these moments that we realize the frailty of our own strength and the inadequacy of our own resources.

God's provision is not based on our own merit or ability. It is a gift He gives freely out of His goodness and mercy. It is easy to be lulled into a false sense of security and complacency by the fleeting comfort of this world. We may think we are in control, but the truth is that we are constantly dependent upon God's grace.

The Lord is our Shepherd. He provides for our needs and sustains us. Prosperity and peace come from God alone. When we realize this truth, our lives change. We can rest in the assurance that God cannot and will not ever fail us.

We must base our mental well-being on the truth of God's Word and confess our sins to God, asking Him to minister to us. Take this moment to dwell on the peace and provision of God in your life and thank Him for the valleys He has delivered you from and the prosperity He has provided to you.

Ask God to give you the strength to reach your full potential, to enable you to complete the tasks before you, and to empower your walk with His joy. Trust that He has good plans for you, plans not to harm you, but to prosper you and give you a hope and a future.

God is enough. He provides for all our needs, both physical and spiritual. He gives us peace and prosperity in our lives. We must choose to rest in the assurance of His Word.

PRAYER

God, I praise You because You always finish what You start. I worship You for the power of Your Word, which transforms and renews my mind. I sing praises to Your name, for You hold the universe in the palm Your hand. I worship You in the knowledge that You work out all things for the good of those who love You. Amen.

Speaking Life

Words can bring death or life! Talk too much,
and you will eat everything you say.

PROVERBS 18:21 CEV

In life, we often face difficult situations that can be challenging to navigate. When things get tough, it is easy to fall into the trap of self-pity and to complain about our circumstances. However, as believers in Christ, we are called to a higher standard of conduct. We are called to speak life over ourselves and not give in to negativity.

As the Scriptures remind us, our words have power, and what we say can either bring life or death. Therefore, it is essential to be intentional about the words we speak over ourselves. When we speak words of encouragement, we align our minds with the mind of Christ, which enables us to overcome any obstacle that comes our way.

It is also essential to speak God's Word over ourselves and declare His promises. We need to remind ourselves that we are more than conquerors in Christ, and all things are possible to those who believe. By speaking these words over ourselves, we can shift our perspective and begin to see our circumstances through God's eyes.

Sometimes we may struggle with controlling our tongues and may have spoken ill words over ourselves and others. In such moments, we need to confess our sins to the Lord and ask for His forgiveness. We must ask God to break the negative words spoken over our lives and empower us to speak life instead.

Choose to speak life over yourself and those around you. Declare God's blessings over your life and trust in His promises. Align your words with God's Word and reap the fruit of your positive confessions. As you speak life over yourself, you will experience God's peace and victory in every area of your life.

PRAYER

Lord, I praise You for everything You have spoken over me and my life. Your Word stands true throughout the ages. I worship You for giving me the ability to speak life, for creating me in Your image, and giving me the authority to speak to my circumstances, in Jesus's name. Amen.

God-Given Power

*My dear children, you belong to God
and have defeated them; because God's Spirit,
who is in you, is greater than the devil, who is in the world.*

1 JOHN 4:4 NCV

God's power is an incredible force that is available to all of us. It is not dependent on our own personal strength or abilities, but it is a gift we can access through our faith in Jesus Christ. *Webster's Dictionary* defines *power* as the "ability to act or to produce an effect." As Christians, we can tap into God's power to overcome any obstacle or challenge that comes our way.

In a world where power often determines victory or defeat, we can take comfort in the fact that our personal power may be small and limited, but we are guaranteed victory through the power of God. This power is greater than anything we will ever face in this world, and it is manifested through the Holy Spirit within us.

God can open doors that are closed and close doors that are open. He can stop evil in its tracks and break generational curses. Through grace and by faith, Jesus extends His victory at the cross of Calvary to us, and we can rest assured that we will also be victorious because God makes His victory our own.

It can be easy to forget this truth when we are facing difficult situations, but we must remember that we are stronger than any opposition because our strength comes from Christ. By adopting a God-given mindset, we can look at the world from a positive perspective and have the assurance of Christ's victory as our guarantee.

If you are struggling to fully receive this truth, let the Holy Spirit minister to the areas of your heart where His assurance does not yet reign. Reflect on God's victories in your life, remembering how it felt to know you are loved and accepted and rejoicing in the grace provided by the blood of Christ.

Through the Holy Spirit, you can ask for the conviction of truth and enablement to have faith in God's Word of victory for your life. You can be filled with His affirmation that you are more than a conqueror in Christ and choose to persevere in the knowledge that like Christ, you, too, will be victorious.

Be filled with the goodness of Christ today and watch as that goodness transforms your life. May you always remember that God's power is available to you, and that you can trust in His victory to overcome any obstacle or challenge that comes your way.

PRAYER

Lord, I praise You, for You know the end before the beginning. I praise You, for You have made a way for me to be called a child of God. I worship You, for You have prepared a table before me in the presence of my enemies. I praise You, for You have gone before me and made a way. Nothing and no one is greater than You. Amen.

**SECTION:
STAYING ON TRACK**

Putting God First

Love GOD, your God,
with your whole heart:
love Him with all that's in you,
love Him with all you've got!

DEUTERONOMY 6:5 THE MESSAGE

God must always come first in our lives. This is not an option; it is a requirement for a fulfilling and fruitful relationship with Him. He demands and commands the first place in our hearts, minds, and bodies. When we allow something or someone else to come before God, we begin to compromise and make concessions that will eventually affect our faith.

To remain strong and steadfast in our relationship with God, we must examine our motivations and seek Him continuously. If we are not sure whether our desire is truly to put Him first, we must confess this to God and seek the comfort of the Holy Spirit.

As you take this moment in His presence, consider the blessing of God's preeminence in your life. Remember how much He loves you and what He sacrificed—for you. Take a posture of gratitude that He watches over you and works in your favor. Thank Him for the ability to know Him and to lead others as you are led by Him.

Jesus gave all of Himself for us on the cross, and we must give all of ourselves to Him in return. We must ask God for the ability to commit ourselves to His service each day—completely and willingly. To remain faithful and true to God, we can't put Him in second place. We must love Him *fully* with all our heart, soul, and strength. We let ourselves decrease and Christ in us increase. We draw our strength from Him as we pour ourselves out for other people.

Choose this very day to give God the first spot in your life. Choose this day to live a life of obedience, in a personal and committed relationship with God. You will see God's goodness and grace manifested in your life, not only today—but in all the days to come.

> **PRAYER**
>
> *Father God, I worship You, for You are who You say You are. Jesus Christ, I praise You for Your unending love. And dear Holy Spirit, I adore You for your relentless kindness. Your patience and Your wisdom have ministered continuously to me. Lord, I bless Your name for there is none like You and no one beside You. Amen.*

Watch What You Do

Don't you realize that your body is the temple of the Holy Spirit, who lives in you and was given to you by God? You do not belong to yourself, for God bought you with a high price. So you must honor God with your body.

I CORINTHIANS 6:19–20 NLT

When we walk with Jesus, we are called to be careful of our actions. We belong to God, and He lives within us. Our bodies are not meant for sin, but they are to be set apart for His purposes. We need to be mindful of where we go and what we do, as our actions can draw us closer to God or take us farther away from Him.

Also, the Holy Spirit lives within our bodies, so we need to treat our bodies with the utmost respect. Everything we do is done before God, and He sees all of it. As the Bible says, when we sow into our flesh, we reap destruction; but when we sow into the Spirit, we reap life.

God has given us free will, and so it is up to us to choose whether we want to bring glory to Him with our bodies or not. We need to be mindful of what is currently being nurtured within us and confess all our negative thoughts and emotions to Him.

With a heart of gratitude, we should also thank God for His wisdom and His Word, which never fail us. His teachings are always for our good, and we should thank Him for keeping our hearts safe and filling us with faith and wisdom. The Holy Spirit will lead us and guard our hearts from arrogance and pride. Our bodies are a temple for the Holy Spirit, and therefore we should honor God with our bodies, making good choices concerning what we do and where we go and watching God's goodness displayed in our lives and in our relationship with Him.

Throughout this day before you, remember to be careful of your actions, knowing that you belong to God and that He lives within you. Strive to sanctify your body and avoid engaging in sin. Ask the Holy Spirit to lead you and help you to make good choices—choices that will bring glory to God.

PRAYER

God, I praise You for gifting me with Your Holy Spirit. I give You my adoration, for only You are just and righteous. Goodness and grace are found in You alone. I worship You, thanking You for the gift of salvation, for the price You paid for my soul. You teach me wisdom in love; Your ways are righteous and true. Amen.

Seek God First

Those who live following their sinful selves
think only about things that their sinful selves want.
But those who live following the Spirit
are thinking about the things the Spirit wants them to do.

ROMANS 8:5 NCV

As we navigate this race of life on earth, it's important to remember that we cannot do it alone. We need the guidance, strength, and wisdom that only the Holy Spirit can provide. In order to have more of the Holy Spirit in our lives, we must seek Him out. We can engage with Him through the things that please Him and invite His presence into our world.

Our flesh and our spirit are like two muscles, and whichever we stretch, exercise, and nourish is the one that will work better. It's easy to give in to our flesh and allow it to become our default state. However, if we learn to submit to the Spirit, we will be able to deny our flesh and feed our spirit. The Holy Spirit is the Companion sent by Jesus to help us accomplish this. He sustains us and encourages us along the way.

It is important not to turn away from the Holy Spirit, as it will be impossible to serve God in the long term without Him. We should instead let Him lead and guide us into righteousness. Take some time to dwell on the importance of God's Spirit and thank Him for the Holy Spirit's presence in your life.

Every day you have the choice to act according to God's Spirit or your own flesh. Ask God for an outpouring of His Spirit, and for the strength to live as Christ lived. When you live according to the Spirit, you are thinking about the things the Spirit wants you to do, and your life will be transformed as you live in fellowship with Him.

So seek after the things of the Spirit and lean on the Holy Spirit to guide you and lead you with godly justice. With the Holy Spirit's guidance, you can stay on track in your race here on earth and live a life that honors and pleases God.

PRAYER

Lord, I give You praise, for You are just and perfect in all Your ways. I worship You for Your unwavering love, for Your grace that covers me. I adore You, Lord, for You are faithful and true. I praise You for Your eternal kingdom, for Your reign, which will know no end. Amen.

Perseverance

The temptations in your life are no different from what others experience. And God is faithful. He will not allow the temptation to be more than you can stand. When you are tempted, He will show you a way out so that you can endure.

I CORINTHIANS 10:13 NLT

Perseverance is a vital aspect of our journey as we follow Christ. It's not always easy to press on when the trials of life seem overwhelming, but we can hold on to the promise that God will always be with us. We cannot be manipulated nor deceived by our circumstances. Instead, we must trust in God's faithfulness and lean on the Holy Spirit to uphold us in our trials.

It's easy to become discouraged and tempted to give up in the midst of trying circumstances, but endurance is cultivated in these times. We can confess our doubts and negative thoughts to God and lay our sins before Him. Through perseverance, we can experience growth and learning, and we can see the blessings that come from righteousness.

Jesus promises wonderful, eternal outcomes to those who endure, and we can focus on these promises during times of trial. Thank God for His grace and for His presence today, even as you walk through difficulties.

The Holy Spirit is available to help us persevere, and we must ask for His help in increasing our faith and making us more like Jesus. We can be confident in the Lord's promise of deliverance and live our lives according to His Word. As we persevere, we will see God's grace manifested in our lives. We will be able to overcome whatever is before us and ultimately receive strength for the journey. So let us not give up, but instead, let us run the race set before us with perseverance, knowing that God is with us every step of the way.

PRAYER

Lord, I praise You, for Your Word is upright and eternal. Your ways are perfect, and all Your works are done in faithfulness. I worship You, for You are a God of fidelity and consistency. You are the merciful God, gracious and righteous in all Your ways. Amen.

Behave Yourself!

Do not give the devil a way to defeat you.

EPHESIANS 4:27 NCV

It is so critical that we are watchful and vigilant of our behavior. Our words and actions have the power to either glorify God or give the enemy a foothold in our lives. Therefore, we must be careful to avoid anything that goes against God's Word.

When we accept Jesus Christ as our Lord and Savior, we are called to a life of righteousness. We are to leave behind our old ways and adopt the ways of Christ. This transformation requires us to renew our minds in the Word and seek the Holy Spirit to help us become more like Him.

The Bible warns us not to give the devil an opportunity to accuse us or move against us. We should not give him any chance to enter our lives—at all. We must stop engaging in sinful behavior such as stealing, gossiping, or being jealous of or hateful to others.

When we seek after the Spirit and avoid ungodly desires, we become more like Christ. However, if we indulge in sinful behavior, our flesh will control us. It is important to remember that we have the power to choose whether to obey God or follow the ways of the enemy.

If you find yourself struggling with sinful behavior, do not despair. Confess your sins to God and ask for His forgiveness. He is willing to extend His grace and mercy to those who seek Him—including you!

Always be thankful for God's goodness in your life. Remember His past blessings and thank Him for all He has done and will continue to do. He is more than capable of helping us become who He has called us to be.

As you approach God, do so boldly, knowing that He loves you and is eager to help you. Ask for His wisdom and knowledge, and for the Holy Spirit to teach you to be vigilant with your thoughts, words, and behavior. Stay watchful and wise and honor the trust God has placed upon you. Avoid anything that would give the enemy a foothold in your life. By doing so, you bring honor to the name of Christ and glorify God.

> **PRAYER**
>
> *Jesus, I praise You, for You alone are good, and Your goodness knows no end. I worship You for Your unfailing righteousness and Your unending grace toward me. I bless Your name, for there is none like You—Your extravagant love sustains me and lifts me up, every day of my life. Amen.*

Find Your Strength in God

*Give yourselves completely to God.
Stand against the devil, and the devil will run from you.*

JAMES 4:7 NCV

Being obedient to God and standing firm in His strength is the key to overcoming the lies we are sometimes tempted to believe. When we lean on the Lord and on His promises, submitting to Him as our source of strength, we find hope. It is only by submitting to Him and obeying His commands that we can access His power and strength.

John 10:10 tells us that the devil is a cunning adversary who is always looking for ways to steal, kill, and destroy us. He has been perfecting his strategies for a long time, and he knows how to get us off track. However, when we stand under God's authority, Satan will flee from us. The Lord of heaven's armies will back us up when we serve Him wholeheartedly.

We cannot overcome Satan on our own, but we can do all things through Christ who strengthens us. Only by surrendering to God's will and following the leading of His Holy Spirit can we create a situation in which Satan knows he cannot win. We must confess our sins before God and remove every foothold of the enemy in our lives.

Consider for a moment God's amazing gift of strength and thank Him for His mercy and grace in your own life. Jesus Christ is the perfect example of how to persevere and rely upon the Father.

He set aside His own personal desires for the benefit of mankind, and He submitted Himself in obedience to God's will.

As we ask the Holy Spirit to help us submit our whole hearts to Christ, we are not alone. Jesus was intimately acquainted with the task of resisting Satan, and He overcame the devil in the strength of His Father. We, too, can overcome the attacks of the enemy by standing firm in the strength of Christ.

Let us give ourselves to God every day and in every way. As we submit to Him and obey His commandments, we will access His power and strength, and Satan will flee from us. The victory is already ours in Christ. Fear not, for He who is in us is greater than he who is in the world!

PRAYER

Dear heavenly Father, I look to You and praise You for Your greatness and Your power. I worship You for the deliverance found in Your presence. I praise You for overcoming the world. God, I bless Your name, for through the blood of Your Son, Jesus, You have made Your victory my own. Amen.

No Turning Back

Jesus said,
"Anyone who begins to plow a field
but keeps looking back
is of no use in the kingdom of God."

LUKE 9:62 NCV

In our walk with God, we are called to give our whole selves over to Him. We cannot hold on to our old ways and expect to serve in the kingdom of heaven. We must let go of our past and press on toward Jesus Christ.

The desires of the flesh are constantly in opposition to the things of the Spirit. We must choose whether we will serve our own desires or submit to God. We cannot serve both! We must present ourselves before the Lord, confess our sins, and put our faith in Him. When we trust God with our restoration, He can rebuild the ruins and bring beauty from ashes. God has the strength we need to persevere and stay on track. As we thank Him for His grace and mercy, He gives our lives purpose and focus, and He teaches us discipline and determination.

Today, as you feel His Spirit move upon your heart, ask God to grant you His grace, to give you the ability to let go of the past, and to teach you to lean on Him instead of on your own understanding. Seek what God has for your life and allow the Holy Spirit to fortify your spirit.

God has called us to let go of the past and to press on toward Jesus Christ. He will enable and empower us through His Holy

Spirit to persevere and run our race through to the finish line. We were not created to live in the past. We must choose to step into the future God has for us, confident in His Word and the power of His grace, today and always.

> **PRAYER**
>
> *Jesus, I adore You in the beauty of Your holiness. I praise You for the wondrous gift of Your salvation through grace. I worship You for Your sacrifice, made at the cross of Calvary, for my own redemption, which was bought with Your precious blood. I give all glory and honor to You alone. In this moment, I ask for Your grace to let go of my past and to press on toward the prize You have for me in Jesus Christ. Help me to be fully committed and submitted to You. I thank You for Your grace and mercy and for giving my life purpose and focus. Amen.*

SECTION:
SPIRITUAL FITNESS

Spiritual Well-Being

*Jesus said, "Yes, I am the vine;
you are the branches.
Those who remain in Me,
and I in them, will produce much fruit.
For apart from Me you can do nothing."*

JOHN 15:5 NLT

As humans, we often seek to find well-being in the things of this world—money, success, relationships, and the list goes on. However, the truth is that only God can provide us with true spiritual well-being. He has created us with a soul, a body, and a spirit, and it is only through Him that we can experience fullness in all three aspects of our being.

We were created for a purpose and a plan, and that plan includes being rooted in Christ. When we are planted in Jesus, we have access to all the spiritual blessings we will ever need. No matter what storms come our way, we can withstand them because we are drawing from the infinite Source of life: God Himself.

It can be easy to forget this truth or to resist accepting it. We get caught up in the busyness of life, and we forget to take the time to dwell on God's promise that He is always with us. But when we open ourselves up to the Holy Spirit, He will fill us with His peace and love.

As you go through your day, you can choose to be rooted in Christ. Ask the Lord to nourish and sustain you, to let your roots run deep in Him, to bless you with multiplication and much fruit.

When you remain in Christ, everything you are and all you do will be rooted in Him.

Choose this day to reach out to the Lord Jesus for His guidance and care. Wait on Him and be blessed by His Spirit on this day and all days to come.

PRAYER

O God, I will sing of Your strength; I will sing out loud of Your steadfast love. For You have been to me a fortress and a refuge in the day of my distress, and my spirit rejoices in Christ, my Savior. Holy Spirit, I know that in Your hands I can rest assured, for You will teach me and guide me. You will keep me safe from all evil. Amen.

Constant Transformation

Let the Spirit
renew your thoughts and attitudes.

EPHESIANS 4:23 NLT

Believers in Jesus Christ are called to be in a constant state of transformation. This transformation happens when we draw from the well of living water that is God's Word. When we meditate on His Word and allow it to penetrate our souls, we are changed from the inside out. The Bible says that the Word of God is sharper than a double-edged sword, and it is able to separate bone from marrow, soul from spirit. There is no way for us to take in the Word of God without being changed by it!

When we spend time in God's Word, we are allowing our heavenly Father to mold us more and more into the image of Christ. We are allowing the Holy Spirit to create in us the person that we were meant to be. This is a process that requires us to be intentional about our time with God. We must make it a priority to read God's Word, the Bible, and meditate on it each day.

God has given us His Word as a gift. We should be grateful for the wisdom and understanding that He imparts to us through His Holy Spirit, through Jesus's teachings and parables, through all the pages of the Bible, His love letter to us. We experience its creative and transformative power when we meditate on it and ask God to plant it in our hearts.

If you haven't been spending consistent quality time reading the Scriptures, make it a priority today. Ask the Lord for a greater understanding of His Word and for Him to set it on fire in your heart. Willingly submit to the process of His transformation, of becoming more like Christ. May you always draw from the well of living water and be transformed by His Word.

PRAYER

Heavenly Father, I praise You, for Your presence transforms my heart and blesses my life. I thank You for the mercy and power that has been provided through the blood of Jesus, Your Son. His blood saves, restores, and renews my soul—my thoughts and the attitudes of my heart. I thank You for the constant work You are doing in my life. Amen.

Walking in God's Calling and Purpose

[You are] to become a new person. That new person is made to be like God— made to be truly good and holy.

EPHESIANS 4:24 NCV

When you come to believe in Jesus, you are called to walk in God's calling and purpose. This means living a life that is aligned with His will and His ways. But how can you do that? The Bible tells us that as a new creation in Christ, you must rely on the Holy Spirit to cultivate a healthy spiritual life.

Our spiritual life is tied to our relationship with God. Without Him, we cannot be spiritual or righteous. We must come to the Father through Jesus, and only then can we be called children of God.

God has laid out standards for us in His Word, and it is only through the strength given to us by the Holy Spirit that we can meet them. We have all fallen short and will continue to fail, but we remember that through the blood of Jesus, we are called righteous through our faith. We can never be good enough to merit salvation on our own.

As we seek God through reading His Word, spending time in prayer, and communing with the Holy Spirit, we will strengthen our inner man and become the new creation we are meant to be.

We must draw near to Him and confess our sins, receiving the free forgiveness offered in Jesus.

Dwell on the new creation you have become in Christ and thank Him for it. Stand on the promise of His Word and ask the Holy Spirit to help you and strengthen you. Ask for the self-control to nourish your spirit and turn away from temptation.

As you make time for Jesus, read your Bible and pray. And as you spend time in God's presence, you will have the great joy of watching Him transform your life. Trust in His plans for you—they are better than you could ever imagine!

PRAYER

Lord, I praise You, for You are a holy and righteous God. I worship You, for Your ways are just and true. I adore You, Holy Spirit, for manifesting God's grace and judgment upon my life. I bless Your holy name! Amen.

Constant Vigilance

Stay alert!
Watch out for your great enemy, the devil.
He prowls around like a roaring lion,
looking for someone to devour.

I PETER 5:8 NLT

Constant vigilance is required for those who follow Christ. We live in a world that is trying to distract us. We must be mindful of what we do, what we say, where we go, and who we allow to influence us. We must guard our eyes and be watchful of what we allow to affect us.

Satan, our adversary, roams the earth looking for those who are ready to stumble. But if he is not successful, as he wasn't with Jesus, he will retreat, hoping for a more opportune time to creep into our hearts. Until we are in heaven to spend eternity with Christ, Satan will not stop coming for us, because we have something he never will—the ability to commune with the ruling power of the universe and to be called His child.

On this day, thank God for the many times He delivered you from the enemy's hand. Recall how God's Word upheld you in times of weakness and how the Holy Spirit strengthened you in times of weariness. Continue to seek God's presence in times of trouble, turning to Him and not to the pleasures the world offers. Choose to be influenced by God and His Word, and you will never be caught unaware by the enemy.

Stay aware, guarding your heart and mind from the attacks of the enemy. Seek God's presence each day and allow Him to guide you and protect you. Choose to be influenced by God and His Word, and you will live a victorious life in Christ!

> **PRAYER**
>
> *God, I praise You and give glory to Your great name. Jesus, I worship You, for You wear the victor's crown. You overcame it all, and You are seated in the highest place. Holy Spirit, I thank You for helping me be aware of the world's influence, turning instead to God's Word. Amen.*

Walking in the Spirit

So I say, let the Holy Spirit guide your lives. Then you won't be doing what your sinful nature craves. The sinful nature wants to do evil, which is just the opposite of what the Spirit wants. And the Spirit gives us desires that are the opposite of what the sinful nature desires. These two forces are constantly fighting each other, so you are not free to carry out your good intentions. But when you are directed by the Spirit, you are not under obligation to the law of Moses.

GALATIANS 5:16–18 NLT

What does it mean to walk in the Spirit and not by the flesh? It is actually pretty simple: we should allow the Holy Spirit to guide us in all that we do. Our thoughts, actions, and words should be led by God, and we must be in constant submission to His will.

The life God calls us to live on this earth is not always an easy one. It requires discipline, sacrifice, and a willingness to be led by a living God who does not always act in predictable ways. However, when we submit to His leading, we are strengthened in our spirits, and we "put to death" the desires of the flesh, which lead to heartbreak, misery, and separation from God.

King David is a great example of someone who constantly sought God's guidance in his life. He would seek God's counsel on many decisions, and God would provide him with specific instructions. This is the type of relationship that God desires to have with each one of us.

If you are struggling today with a decision, unsure of what to do, bring your worries to Christ. Take up His burden, confess your sins, and receive His forgiveness. Consider the Holy Spirit's leading and thank God for it. Thank Him for His holy Word and for providing a gentle, loving Counselor to guide you each day.

Remember that living by the Spirit means that you will not do what your sinful self wants. This may be difficult at first, but over time, you will become more disciplined. Be encouraged—you have God's Holy Spirit to show you the way and to assist you.

Today ask Him for help in submitting your spirit to His, for God to strengthen you so you might turn away from temptation, and for Him to give you the ability to follow His will. Be led by the Spirit and walk in His ways, for in doing so, you will experience spiritual well-being and be blessed with a closer relationship with your loving Father.

PRAYER

Lord, I praise You, for in Your presence, there is fullness of joy. Jesus, I thank You for the grace that enables me to have fellowship with the Holy Spirit. Holy Spirit, I worship You for empowering me to live a godly life and to walk in full victory over the enemy. Amen.

Your Body Is a Holy Offering

I urge you, brothers and sisters, in view of God's mercy,
to offer your bodies as a living sacrifice, holy and pleasing to God—
this is your true and proper worship.

ROMANS 12:1 NIV

The Bible teaches us that our bodies are temples of the Holy Spirit (see I Corinthians 6:19–20). Because of this, it is essential that we are mindful of how we conduct ourselves in this physical world, as it affects our spiritual well-being. Our daily actions impact our relationship with God, and so we must strive to live in accordance with His will.

Our thoughts and actions are interlinked. Our thoughts influence our actions, which directly affect our relationship with God. Therefore, we must make a conscious effort to ensure that our thoughts and actions are pure and draw us closer to God.

God desires victory for us, not defeat. However, we cannot achieve this victory on our own. We must seek the Holy Spirit's strength to overcome the flesh and live in constant communication with God. Through the confession of our sins and submission to the Holy Spirit, we can experience victory over the flesh and walk in the Spirit.

Our bodies were made to worship God. Through Christ, we are given the path to forgiveness and grace. We offer our lives as living sacrifices to Him by pursuing godly things. When our bodies, souls, and spirits are knit together in harmony, we can live securely in His presence and experience constant companionship with the Holy Spirit.

Take a moment to thank God for the sacrifice of His Son, Jesus, which made it possible for us to come before Him spotless and righteous. Let us also thank the Holy Spirit for drawing near to us, encouraging us, and comforting us in times of trouble and temptation.

As you go through your daily life, stay mindful of your conduct and strive to live in accordance with God's will. Serve the Lord with your body, offering it as a holy sacrifice, pleasing and acceptable to Him.

> **PRAYER**
>
> *Heavenly Father, I praise You, for You are Lord over all the earth and the heavens. Jesus, I thank You for Your love, which made a way for me to know You. Holy Spirit, I worship You for enabling me to live according to God's righteousness and empowering me to walk in the fullness of God's goodness and His grace. Amen.*

Your Spiritual Health

Do not follow foolish stories that disagree
with God's truth, but train yourself to serve God.
Training your body helps you in some ways,
but serving God helps you in every way
by bringing you blessings in this life
and in the future life, too.

I TIMOTHY 4:7–8 NCV

As human beings, we tend to focus on our physical health and our mental well-being. We work out, eat healthy food, and seek therapy to take care of ourselves. However, what many people don't realize is that the key to our overall well-being lies in our spiritual health.

It is easy to overlook the importance of our spiritual lives. We often neglect this aspect of ourselves and focus on other parts of our lives. But the truth is that a strong spiritual life affects every area of our existence. Our physical, mental, and emotional health all depend on our spiritual health.

It is crucial to exercise our spiritual muscles daily and constantly. We do this by reading the Word of God, spending time with Him in prayer and worship, and cultivating a relationship with the Holy Spirit. We seek salvation through Jesus Christ and confess our sins before Him to refresh our spirits.

When you take a moment to dwell on God's importance in your life, you can thank Him for His power, provision, grace, attentive care, unending lovingkindness, and protection. You can also ask for His help, strength, and empowerment through the Holy Spirit.

Serving God is not only beneficial to our spiritual health, but also to our lives here on earth and in eternity to come.

Your spiritual health is the key to your overall well-being. So prioritize it, exercise your spiritual muscles daily, and seek God in every area of your life. Continue to serve Him and pursue all that He has for you, both now and in the future.

PRAYER

God, I praise You, for there is none like You. You have set eternity within the human heart, and You have given us the chance to prepare for it. Jesus, I worship You. Your blood paved the way for the eternal restoration of all mankind, and Your grace grants us access to the Holy Spirit. I praise Your name, Lord, for You alone are worthy of all honor and glory. Amen.

SECTION:
BECOMING PRESENT

God's Progressive Work

God is the one who began this good work in you, and I am certain that He won't stop before it is complete on the day that Christ Jesus returns.

PHILIPPIANS 1:6 CEV

God's work is progressive, but as humans, our vision and understanding are limited. We cannot see things the way God sees them, and we do not know all the plans He has for us or how He will bring them to pass. However, we can be assured that God's work in our lives *will* be completed.

Sometimes we become stagnant in our pursuits, and our dreams begin to weigh us down, making it difficult to move forward. We may start to impose our timelines and ideas onto God's work, causing us to become frustrated and discouraged when things do not happen the way we planned. During these moments, it is essential to cling to our faith and avoid allowing the lies in.

Transformation is a progressive process that takes time, and we must not become discouraged with what we perceive as a lack of progress. Instead of allowing our past to hold us back, we should surrender control to God and allow Him to work His grace and mercy in our lives.

It is crucial to reflect on God's faithfulness and the wonders He has done in our lives. We can recall the times when we chose to trust in His promises and thank Him for His peace, which surpasses all understanding. God is present, and He is continually making our ways straight.

In addition, Jesus promised to send the Holy Spirit to be with us always, so we are never alone. We can pray for His presence to permeate every area of our lives, increase our faith, and teach us to trust even when we cannot see what lies ahead.

Keeping all this in mind, do not be anxious or afraid, for God knows what He has for you, and He is not limited by your past. You can trust that He will keep His Word and finish everything He has started in your life. Surrender your control to God and trust in His perfect plan for you—it is good!

PRAYER

I exalt You, Lord, for You finish everything You begin! You are the God of all people, and by Your word, I was created. I adore You, who formed all my days and who holds everything in the palm of Your hands. You know the end before the beginning. You turn my ashes into beauty and my mourning into dancing. Amen.

Entrusting Your Future to God

Trust in the LORD with all your heart;
do not depend on your own understanding.
Seek His will in all you do,
and He will show you which path to take.

PROVERBS 3:5–6 NLT

Life is full of uncertainties, and it is natural to worry about the future. We tend to question our decisions and wonder how they will affect our destiny. We overthink and overanalyze ourselves, and this can sometimes lead us into oblivion. However, as believers, we know that we don't have to carry the burden of our future alone. We have a heavenly Father who is ready to guide us and take us where we need to go. The Bible tells us to entrust our future to God.

Trusting God with our future means relinquishing control and allowing Him to take the wheel. It means acknowledging that His ways are higher than ours and that His vision is greater and wider than ours. It means having faith that He is who He says He is and that we are who He says we are. When we put our trust in God and allow the Holy Spirit to lead us, we can be present and live each day to the fullest. We can enjoy the journey and be confident that God is in control.

God's work in our lives is progressive, and He will finish what He started. We have faith that He is near to us in every moment and that He has good plans for our future. We don't have to live in fear of yesterday or be anxious about tomorrow because God is with us today. He is our promise now and our assurance for the days to come.

So today, seek God's direction in your life and trust Him with your future. Have faith that He will show you where to go when you listen for His guidance. Thank Him for moving mountains and for preparing good plans for your future. Trust that He will never lead you astray and that He wants to bless you this day and all other future days to come. May you always remember that you are not alone, and may you have the courage to always entrust your future to God.

PRAYER

Jesus, I praise You, for You are the way, the truth, and the life. No one comes to the Father except through You. I adore You because Your Word is a light to my path. I worship You, for You alone have power and dominion over all the earth. You are in control of everything and every circumstance—including my own life. I trust You, Lord. Amen.

True Contentment

*You will show me the way of life,
granting me the joy of Your presence and
the pleasures of living with You forever.*

PSALM 16:11 NLT

Contentment is not something we can attain through our own efforts. It is found in God alone. As we seek God's presence and commit our lives to living in the constancy of the Holy Spirit, we will experience joy and pleasure beyond what we could ever imagine.

God has designated a path for us to follow so we can live life to its fullest. This path is in the presence of God, at the feet of Jesus, and in the Holy Spirit. As we commit our lives to seeking God's presence, all other things will be added unto us. We do not need to attract happiness or material wealth, but instead, we need to allow ourselves to be attracted to the heavenly Father, the Giver of all the good gifts we experience here on earth.

In this moment, you can dwell on the life God has prepared for you. You can think of past situations in which you have delighted in His presence and thank the Holy Spirit for showing you the path that leads to life. You can appreciate the pleasures He has allowed you to experience—and look forward to more! No matter the season in which you find yourself, you can always seek God and delight in His presence.

As we ask God to help us find contentment in our daily activities, to give us an appreciation for the wonder of His creation, and to guide our steps toward the path of life, we can trust that He will teach us His way to live. Jesus died to give us a life filled with joy and pleasure, and the Holy Spirit is here to show us how to live, to help us find what will truly make us happy.

Let's not waste the precious time we have today looking for things that won't bring fulfillment, but instead, let's look toward God and trust that true contentment and fulfillment lie in His presence alone. May we seek the Lord while He may be found and delight in His presence always!

PRAYER

God, I give You praise, for Your Word is eternal. You are the Source of my joy, my strength, and my salvation. God, You are so good, and all good gifts come from You. In Your presence, I find everything I need. I praise You because You are the everlasting God, who has prepared an eternal home for me. Amen.

Seek Him First

Search for the LORD and for His strength;
continually seek Him.

I CHRONICLES 16:11 NLT

Human beings often spend their lives chasing after things that don't matter in the grand scheme of things. We place so much importance on our possessions, material things, or fleeting moments of entertainment or gossip on social media that we forget to focus on what truly matters. We forget to seek God continuously.

God desires to fill our lives with fullness and joy, and the only way to receive this life and joy is through His Holy Spirit. We cannot live the life God has called us to live without the Holy Spirit. Therefore, we must continually seek His presence.

So many blessings are found in His presence! That is where we find love, grace, correction, forgiveness, and goodness. Whatever we need, we will find it in the presence of the Lord. God sustains us, anchors our souls, resolves our past, plans for our future, and enables us to live in this present world, with all its troubles and pressures.

Perhaps you have been struggling in your relationship with God, maybe even ignoring Him altogether, because you are overwhelmed or busy with so many other things. Regardless of your circumstances, you have the opportunity to fix your situation today. You can present yourself before God boldly and confidently, confess your sin, and trust that everything you need can be found under His sheltering arms.

In addition, remember to thank God for all the past goodness and favor He has bestowed upon your life—and for what is still to come. God is here and listening to your prayers. He never said life would be easy, but He has promised to be there every step of the way. He sent the Holy Spirit to be your Helper, and He wants you to succeed!

Ask the Holy Spirit to help you overcome the stress of this world, press on when life gets rough, and recognize God's mercy in every season of your life. Acknowledge God's goodness every day and in every way. Don't forget that the Lord's love for you never ends, and His mercies are new every morning. You have the Lord, and no matter what you may lose, you still have hope. Even in the midst of hardship, God is still good, and He is still in control. You can live with confidence in God's Word and watch His blessings be poured out into your life.

PRAYER

Heavenly Father, I worship You, for You are the God of gods and the Lord of lords. You are the great, the mighty, and the awesome God. There is nowhere on earth I can flee from Your presence. I praise You, for You will never leave me nor forsake me. You, Jesus, died in my place so that I may always have the Holy Spirit at my side. Amen.

Great Things Ahead!

Jesus said, "Ask, and God will give to you.
Search, and you will find. Knock, and the door will open for you.
Yes, everyone who asks will receive. Everyone who searches will find.
And everyone who knocks will have the door opened."

MATTHEW 7:7-8 NCV

God's goodness is available to us at every moment, even in the midst of difficult circumstances. It can be easy to lose sight of this truth when we are facing trials or when life is just overwhelming. However, we must remember that Jesus opened the door for us to come before the throne room of God with boldness.

When Jesus died on the cross, the veil in the temple was torn, signifying that the way to heaven was made accessible to us. We are now able to access the Father and seek God's goodness and presence in our lives. It is not because of our own works, but because of Jesus's sacrifice for us that we have this privilege. All we need to do is knock and ask for forgiveness, and it will be given to us.

God is greater than anything we have done in the past, and He can help us overcome it. He is with us in the present, and He holds our future as well. We can trust Him with our lives, as we live in His freedom in the present and seek all He has for us.

As you seek God's presence, ask Him to make you more aware of His presence and help you to hear His voice. You can also ask the Holy Spirit to minister the truth of His Word in your heart and enable you to be present in every moment of your life.

Never be afraid to knock on the door of God's presence. Jesus has made a way for us, and we can expect Him to answer us and bless us beyond measure. We can thank God for the privilege of being able to pray to Him whenever we wish and for Him always hearing us. Continue asking, searching, and knocking—and God will answer. If you persevere in seeking His presence, you will be able to live every moment in His presence.

> **PRAYER**
>
> *God, I praise You, for You allow us into Your presence, despite our imperfections. You delight when we seek You in our weakness and need. I worship You, for You answer me when I call; You are not a distant God I cannot reach. I give You praise, for You do what You say and; what You say, You fulfill. Your promises are faithful and sure! Amen.*

Maintaining Joy

Be joyful in hope,
patient in affliction, faithful in prayer.

ROMANS 12:12 NIV

In life, we are bound to face various seasons, some good and some not so good. It is easy to be joyful and grateful when everything is going well, but what about when things take a turn for the worse? How do we maintain our joy when our circumstances are challenging?

The good news is that we can have joy in all seasons. Joy is not the same as happiness, which is dependent on external factors. Joy, on the other hand, is a deep-seated contentment that comes from knowing and trusting God. Our joy is rooted deep in God, our Rock. He is the unchanging foundation upon which we can build our lives.

When we face difficult times, we can still find joy that springs from hope. We have hope in Jesus, who has promised to be with us always, even to the end of the age. He is the same yesterday, today, and forever. We can trust Him to see us through whatever challenges we may face.

In times of trouble, we can be patient and steadfast, knowing that God is with us. We must also never stop praying, even when we feel like giving up. God is always listening and always faithful to answer our prayers. We can be assured that the Holy Spirit is with us, even in our darkest moments, and that Jesus is waiting for us at the finish line.

Take comfort in the fact that you are not alone. God longs for you to feel His joy and to be sustained by His hope. You can ask the Holy Spirit to fill you with His rivers of living water, to strengthen you in your faith, and to pray for you when you cannot pray for yourself. You can trust that God has amazing blessings in store for you, both in this life and for all eternity!

So, practice finding joy in Jesus Christ today, regardless of your circumstances. Trust in God and hold on to the hope that you have in Him. Be patient and steadfast, and never stop praying. God is faithful, and He will sustain you through every season of your life!

PRAYER

Jesus Christ, the faithful and true Savior, I worship You and bless Your name. You know the trials and temptations that I face, and You give me the strength to overcome them. You steady my heart and my mind; You lift up my weary head. Jesus, You are the good Shepherd of my soul; You sustain me at all times. You fill my heart with rejoicing and my mouth with praise. Amen.

Our Constant, Unchanging God

Jesus Christ is the same yesterday, today, and forever.

HEBREWS 13:8 NLT

The Lord never changes. This is a truth that we can hold on to no matter what season of life we find ourselves in. Our circumstances may shift, our emotions may fluctuate, but God remains constant. His promises are true for all who believe in Him.

We can have assurance in God because He will never abandon us. We can trust in Him, and we can hold His words close to our hearts. His promises will never fail, and His Word endures past the end of the ages.

As we reflect on God's unchanging nature, we can find joy in the knowledge that He is always with us. We can give thanks for the moments when He has ministered to our hearts and for the blessings of past seasons. And we can have hope for the future, secure in the knowledge that God is by our side.

In your time with God today, ask for His unchanging nature to provide you with peace. Ask the Holy Spirit to increase your faith and trust in God's promises for your life. And decide today to experience a day free of stress and anxiety, confident of God's presence that is always with you.

We can be assured that Jesus Christ is the same yesterday, today, and forever. He never changes—and that is good news! He is good, faithful, and *always* enough. In every season of life, we can be confident that *God's got us*. So let us choose to live our lives with Him, trusting in His unchanging nature and living in the joy and peace that only He can provide.

> **PRAYER**
>
> *Jesus, I praise You, for You never change. You knew me before I was knit together in my mother's womb. Your plans and purposes were formed before I was, and You will be with me as I see those plans come to fruition in my life. I give You all glory and honor, Jesus, for You are the Author and the Finisher of my faith. May Your name be praised forevermore! Amen.*

SECTION: SUSTAINED FAITH

True Belief in God

Faith means being sure of the things we hope for and knowing that something is real even if we do not see it.

HEBREWS 11:1 NCV

Faith is not just a religious concept; it's a way of life. It is the foundation of our relationship with God and the key to unlocking the fullness of His promises. As believers in Jesus, we are called to have faith, to trust in God's Word, and to believe that He will do what He says He will do.

Sometimes it can be hard to have faith, especially when we are facing difficult circumstances. We may feel overwhelmed by fear and doubt, and we may struggle to see the hand of God at work in our lives. But even in these moments, we must hold on to our faith, knowing that God is with us and that He will never leave us nor forsake us.

Faith is the intangible substance that fuels our relationship with God. It is the foundation upon which we build our lives, the assurance that we are not alone in this world. When we have faith, we can face any challenge with confidence, knowing that God is in control and that He will work all things together for our good.

If you are struggling with unbelief today, know that you are not alone. The good news is that God is always ready and willing to help us in our times of need. All we need to do is ask Him for help and trust that He will come through for us.

Take a moment today to dwell on God's faithfulness. Remember the times when He increased your faith, when you saw His hand at work in your life. Thank Him for His care and steadfastness, and ask Him to help you grow in your faith as you walk closely with Him.

Faith means being sure of the things we hope for. It means knowing that something is real even if we do not see it. So let's hold on to our faith, trusting in God's promises and knowing that He will never let us down.

PRAYER

Jesus, I praise You that You are a Man of Your word. I give You all glory and honor, for there is none like You. You are a covenant-keeping God, and all Your words are true. I worship You, for You are the only One who is worthy of my praise. Lord, Your faithfulness knows no end! Amen.

How Faith Comes

So faith comes from hearing,
and hearing through the word of Christ.

ROMANS 10:17 ESV

Faith is not something that we are born with, nor is it something that we can obtain through our own efforts. Faith is a gift from God that we receive through His Word. As we read and study the Bible, we come to understand who God is, what He has done in the past, and what He can do in our lives today.

The Bible is filled with promises and truths that can sustain us through even the toughest of times. When we fill ourselves up with God's Word, our faith grows stronger and stronger. The Bible tells us to be strong and courageous, for the Lord has done great things for us. This is not just a suggestion or a nice sentiment, but a command from God Himself.

When we read about what God has done in the past, it reminds us that He is capable of doing the same thing in our lives today. Nothing is impossible for Him! As the Word catches fire in our hearts, we begin to understand the mysteries of God revealed to us in Jesus.

Perhaps you have been struggling with finding time or the desire to read your Bible. This is your opportunity to ask God to help you, and He will be delighted to. Confess this need before God and draw near to Him. Ask Him to fill you with faith and to give you the ability to receive and understand His Word with an open heart.

Thank God for the wisdom of His Word, for His strength and His might that are limitless. Thank Him for the promise and the power of His Word that is manifested in your life. Give thanks to God for all the times in the past when His Word ministered to you, when His Word brought courage and faith to your heart.

And as you continue to read and study the Bible, seek to share God's Word with others, and allow others to share God's Word with you. Ask God to help you meditate on and memorize His Word. Take courage and trust that God's Holy Spirit will help you. Do not allow yourself to grow weary of this intimacy with the Holy Spirit; instead, choose to seek God this day and every day.

PRAYER

God, I worship You, for Your faithfulness to me. I adore You, for Your love is unending and unmeasurable. I praise You, for You are gracious and kind; Your forgiveness is vast and inexhaustible. I give You my adoration, for You have made a way for me to be righteous before You. Your Word is a light to my feet and a lamp to my path. Amen.

Meeting God through Our Faith

For I am not ashamed of this Good News about Christ. It is the power of God at work, saving everyone who believes—the Jew first and also the Gentile. This Good News tells us how God makes us right in His sight. This is accomplished from start to finish by faith. As the Scriptures say, "It is through faith that a righteous person has life."

ROMANS 1:16–17 NLT

Faith is not just a mere belief or an intellectual exercise, but a crucial aspect of our relationship with God. It is what enables us to receive the gift of salvation through Jesus Christ. Faith is the key that unlocks the door to a deeper and more meaningful relationship with God.

Living by faith requires a daily commitment to trust in God and in His promises. It means surrendering our doubts, fears, and worries to Him and relying on His strength to see us through difficult times. When we have faith, we can communicate with God through prayer, seeking His guidance and wisdom in all areas of our lives.

Reading God's Word and believing in His promises helps us grow in faith and strengthens our relationship with Him. As we reflect on past experiences when our faith has sustained us, we can thank God for His mercy and faithfulness in our lives. This becomes a wonderful opportunity to lay our hearts bare before Him and ask for an increase in our faith.

Your heavenly Father longs to have a relationship with you, and for you to increase your faith in Him. As you choose to cultivate a life of faith, you will step outside of doubt and move into the amazing future God has for you. With faith as your foundation, you can live with confidence and hope, knowing that the person who is made right with God by faith will live forever in heaven with Him!

> **PRAYER**
>
> *God, I give You praise today. Jesus, You opened the way of salvation to all, and all are welcome at Your table. I worship You, for You are righteous and true. You pour out Your mercy, and with lovingkindness, You attract my heart. I praise You, for You are the everlasting God. Your goodness and Your faithfulness know no end. Amen.*

Pleasing God through Our Faith

Without faith no one can please God.
Anyone who comes to God must believe that He is real
and that He rewards those who truly want to find Him.

HEBREWS 11:6 NCV

Faith is not merely positive vibes or good intentions toward the universe; it is the acknowledgment of the existence of God and our need for Him. Without faith, it is impossible to please Him—to act in a way that brings joy to God. And we cannot have a relationship with someone we do not acknowledge, so to have a relationship with God, we must first believe that He exists.

Once we accept the truth of God's existence and identity, we can have a meaningful relationship with Him. This relationship is crucial if we want to overcome the challenges of this world. But to believe in God, we must first know Him, and the best source of knowledge on Him is His Word. The more we read the Bible, the more we learn about God, and the better our relationship with Him becomes.

God loves us, and He longs to bless us, but we must first believe in Him. If you're struggling to believe the truth of who God is, take this opportunity to approach God and ask Him for help. Ask the Holy Spirit to convict you of the truth of His identity.

Next, reflect on God's love and mercy in your life, and thank Him for it. His love is all-encompassing and has no limits. He affords us constant forgiveness for all our offenses, and He gives us compassion in place of condemnation. Thank Him for past experiences in which His love gifted you with mercy, and thank Him for all the past blessings of His grace over your life and for those still to come.

The Father sent His Son, Jesus, to die for us while we were still lost in our sins, because He believes in the restoration of the relationship between Himself and humanity. Approach His throne of grace today with confidence, knowing who He is and that He loves you. Petition God for His mercy to flood your soul and to increase your faith and assurance in who He really is.

Faith is so important for a meaningful relationship with God. Believe in Him, read His Word, and seek Him with all your heart. Approach Him with confidence and thank Him for His love and mercy in your life. May God increase your faith and draw you closer to Him every day!

PRAYER

God, I praise You for giving me the very best of who You are and for demonstrating Your love through Your actions at the cross. I exalt You, Lord, for Your steadfast faithfulness to me at all times. You withhold nothing, and You give of Yourself freely. Thank You, Lord, that I can always draw near to You. Amen.

Faith Brings Healing

Jesus said to the woman,
"You are now well because of your faith.
May God give you peace! You are healed,
and you will no longer be in pain."

MARK 5:34 CEV

Faith brings healing to whatever ails us. In today's passage, we find a woman who had been sick for twelve years, and her faith in Jesus brought about her healing. Despite all the efforts she had made to find wholeness in her body, nothing had worked until she put her faith in the Lord. She believed that if she could only touch the hem of His garment, she would be healed—and that faith was rewarded.

Like the woman in the story, we, too, may be in need of healing. It may be physical, emotional, or spiritual healing that we require. We may have tried many different things to find healing, but nothing seems to be working. It can be discouraging and disheartening when we don't see the results we desire, especially if we or someone we love is very sick.

Today, we can learn from the woman in the story and put our faith in Jesus. He is our Healer. Believe that He has the power to heal you—and that He is willing to do so. You can reach out to Him today in faith and trust that He will respond.

When we come to Jesus in faith, we are not alone. He is present with us, and He cares deeply about our needs. He understands our struggles and our fears. He knows what it's like to suffer and to feel pain. He is a compassionate and loving Savior, who desires to bring healing to our bodies and our world.

If you or someone you love is in need of healing today, be encouraged to come to Jesus in faith. Reach out to Him and believe in His power to heal. Ask Him to minister to your heart and soul right now. Trust in His love and grace and receive the healing that He has for you.

Faith brings healing. When we put our faith in Jesus, we can experience the power of His love and grace in our lives. We can be made well because we believe. So step out in faith today and touch the hem of Jesus's garment. He is waiting to heal you and to fill you with His peace.

PRAYER

Heavenly Father, I praise You for sending Your Son to sacrifice Himself for me. By His stripes, I am healed, and by His mercy, I am saved. You do not hide Yourself from me, and You always give Your goodness without measure. I sing Your praises, for You make me whole and give me peace. I worship You, for Your lovingkindness has restored me—body and soul. Amen.

Persevere in Your Faith

Fight the good fight of the faith.
Take hold of the eternal life to which you were called
when you made your good confession
in the presence of many witnesses.

I TIMOTHY 6:12 NIV

Perseverance in faith is not an easy task. As we journey through life, we encounter situations that can test our faith, such as the tragic death of loved ones, betrayal from those closest to us, and circumstances we never dreamed we would have to live through. But the race does not stop, and neither can we. We must persevere in our faith and remain faithful to the calling God has entrusted to us.

We are burdened by a glorious purpose in the Kingdom of God, and we must have faith that we are doing a great work that cannot be stopped. It is understandable that this task may seem Herculean and impossible, but we are not alone. Jesus went to the cross, and it was not easy or pleasant for Him, but He understands the pain of perseverance and the exhaustion of endurance. He is waiting for us with open arms, cheering us on, and lending us His strength so that we may overcome—as He did.

Persevering in faith is like running a race, and we must run as hard as we can to win. Our hope is to receive the life that continues forever—because we were called to have that life! We must not hold back but continue to ask for God's strength and help to persevere. We can overcome because Jesus overcame, but we must reach out to God in faith so that we may see the very best of His goodness manifested in our lives.

God never promised that persevering in faith would be easy, but He has promised to help us every step of the way. He sent His Holy Spirit to enable us to overcome all fear, push past doubts, and maintain our trust in Him no matter what. We must ask the Holy Spirit to increase our faith, make us more like Jesus, help us to endure the trials of this world, and empower us to overcome as Jesus did. The plans of our heavenly Father are good, and He is in control!

Continue to persevere in faith and remain faithful to the calling God has entrusted to you. While you need to foster your faith in God and His plans for your life, you should also ask Him to increase your faith and empower you to overcome the challenges you face. You can overcome because Jesus overcame, so thank Him for His example of perseverance in faith and His grace, poured out to you. Reach out to God in faith and see the very best of His goodness manifested in your life.

PRAYER

Jesus, I praise You, for You have not left me alone, but instead, You sent the Holy Spirit to empower me. You have called me and enabled me to run my race, and You have given me eternal life to look forward to—a life forever with You! You sacrificed Yourself to restore my relationship with God the Father. Thank You so much for Your salvation. You alone are worthy of all the praise and glory! Amen.

God Increases Faith

Jesus said, "Those who accept My commandments
and obey them are the ones who love Me.
And because they love Me, My Father will love them.
And I will love them and reveal Myself to each of them."

JOHN 14:21 NLT

Obedience to God's Word is one of the foundational principles of our faith. It is through our obedience that we demonstrate our love for God and deepen our relationship with Him. Our faith is not merely an intellectual pursuit; it is a personal and intimate relationship with the living God, the Creator of the universe!

By loving God and obeying His Word, we invite His presence and personhood into our lives. He becomes our constant companion and guide, and we experience the manifestation of the source of our faith. This deepens our trust in Him and reinforces our belief in His promises.

In moments of uncertainty, fear, and doubt, we must remember who we are in Christ. We are already loved and chosen—and that is truly enough. We can reflect on God's faithfulness and thank Him for His unwavering truth and goodness.

If you struggle to sustain your faith and persevere in God's calling, you can turn to Jesus. He wants you to live a victorious life and to trust Him completely. You can ask the Holy Spirit to transform your mind and teach you how to be obedient, staying confident in the truth that God is who He says He is.

As we choose faith each day, we can be filled with the confidence of Christ and His righteousness. We were created for love, and we experience God's goodness and love through our faith in Him. Let's embrace obedience to God's Word as a way to deepen our relationship with Him and increase our faith today.

PRAYER

I exalt Your name, O God, Most High, for there is no one holy like You. There is no one beside You in all the universe. Jesus, You humbled Yourself so that I might have salvation. You were obedient to the point of death—even death on a cross. I praise You for allowing me to draw near to Your presence. Thank You for never leaving me nor forsaking me. Amen.

> SECTION:
> CONQUER LONELINESS

God Loves You!

*The Lord appeared to us in the past, saying:
"I have loved you with an everlasting love;
I have drawn you with unfailing kindness."*

JEREMIAH 31:3 NIV

God's love for us is beyond measure! It is a love that transcends time and space, a love that existed before we were even created. As human beings, we are limited in our capacity to love. Our love is often conditional, based on certain circumstances or requirements. Our relationships with others can be broken by disagreements, distance, or death. But God's love is different. His love is eternal and unchanging.

It can be difficult to fully comprehend the depth of God's love for us, but we can trust that it is real and unending. The Holy Spirit, who was sent by Jesus to be our Comforter, is always with us, guiding us and reminding us of God's love. Through the Holy Spirit, we are able to experience the peace and comfort that only God can provide.

Jesus did not just die for us so that we could be with God in heaven one day. His death also gave us access to God in the here and now. The Holy Spirit is the one who convicts us of sin, invites us into a relationship with Jesus, and assures us of our salvation when we accept Him as our Savior.

God's love is not something that we have to earn or strive for. It is a gift freely given to us, and all we have to do is accept it. We can come before God, confess our sins, and leave our burdens at His feet. He desires to draw us near and to love us unconditionally.

Today, take a moment to thank God for His lovingkindness. Thank Him for turning His heart toward you while you were yet a sinner, for loving you, and for having a purpose and plan for your life. Give thanks for the times He has ministered to you and drawn you to Himself.

Also pray for the Holy Spirit to fill you with the assurance of your place in God's heart. Ask Him to teach you to trust in God's faithfulness, to know that He will love you beyond time itself!

God's love for us is eternal, and it goes beyond the end of time. He will never stop offering His love to us, and He will never withdraw it. Let's trust in the Lord and hold on to His love with both hands, knowing He will never fail us.

PRAYER

I praise You, God, for Your love outlasts the earth itself. You loved me before I was formed in my mother's womb. Jesus, I worship You, for You offered Yourself in my place before I was born. You loved me while I was yet a sinner, despite my weakness. I worship You, for Your love rescued me and redeemed me. Amen.

God Will Never Abandon You

Even if my father and mother abandon me, the LORD will hold me close.

PSALM 27:10 NLT

Loneliness can be a crushing burden to bear. It is a feeling that can quickly spiral out of control, leaving us feeling isolated and alone. It is in those moments that we need to remember that God will never abandon us. Although we may feel forsaken by those we love, God will never turn His back on us. He will always be there, waiting with open arms to receive us to Himself. It is up to us, though, to choose to trust in His faithfulness, regardless of our circumstances.

When we feel lost or alone, we can turn to God. He is always waiting for us, ready to welcome us into His loving embrace. We need only to call out His name, and He will be right there, ready to comfort and help us. Not only that, but He is always present, listening to our prayers. We can bring our fears and doubts to Him, asking Him to bring peace and healing to our hearts and souls.

Even if you feel abandoned by those closest to you today, you can find solace in the fact that God cares for you. His love knows no bounds, and He will always be there to lift you up when you fall. Choose His love for you! Turn to Him today and trust in His faithfulness, knowing that He will never disappoint. His unwavering love and compassion will surround you, even in the darkest and loneliest of times.

> **PRAYER**
>
> *I praise You, God, for You see all, and nothing is hidden from Your sight. You are near to the brokenhearted, and You give strength to the downtrodden in spirit. Jesus, I worship You, for You never leave me alone. I praise You, Holy Spirit, my constant Companion and Comforter. You will never leave me nor forsake me. Amen.*

Call Upon God

You came near when I called You,
and You said, "Do not fear."

LAMENTATIONS 3:57 NIV

In times of loneliness, it is easy to believe lies. We can feel as if no one hears us, and that even if they did, no one would care. But the truth is, we have a God who is always near to the brokenhearted and who hears their cries for help. There is no place where we can flee from His presence. He is always with us, even when we walk through the valley of the shadow of death—one of the loneliest places to be.

The good news is that we don't need an intermediary, an interpreter, or someone holier than us to talk to God for us. Jesus died to give us free access to God, and He just wants us to come to Him for everything we need. The Holy Spirit is our great Comforter and Counselor, and He is waiting for us to turn to Him in our times of loneliness and despair. We can call out to Him from wherever we are, with confidence He will hear us and answer us.

When we come before God's throne, we don't need to fear rejection. We can confess our sins to Him and receive forgiveness, comfort, and love. We can be so thankful to Him for the access we have to Him and for His desire to care for us!

We can also ask God to help us let go of the anxiety that festers in our hearts, especially when we feel all alone. We can ask Jesus for the ability to rely on His Word for His peace, a peace that surpasses all understanding. We can ask the Holy Spirit to empower us to keep control over our thoughts and emotions, especially when they are trying to convince us of things that are not true.

The Bible tells us we are not to worry. Instead, we are to make our requests known to God through prayer and petition with thanksgiving. So let's set aside all anxiety, fear, and doubt and choose to call on God's name. Let's present our requests before Him and ask for His grace. God is on our side, and He wants to hear our prayers and bless us. So let's be bold and brave and reach out today to receive His peace for our lives.

> **PRAYER**
>
> *I exalt You, Lord, because You fill me with courage and strength. You lift me up on wings like eagles and keep me from stumbling. Jesus, there is none like You, able to save. There is nowhere I can go, neither above the earth or below, where I can escape Your presence. I praise You, God, for You hear me when I call. Your eyes are always upon me. Amen.*

God's Unconditional Love

*I am convinced that nothing can ever separate us from God's love.
Neither death nor life, neither angels nor demons,
neither our fears for today nor our worries about tomorrow—
not even the powers of hell can separate us from God's love.
No power in the sky above or in the earth below—
indeed nothing in all creation will ever be able to separate us
from the love of God that is revealed in Christ Jesus our Lord.*

ROMANS 8:38–39 NLT

God's love is truly unconditional. It is a love that existed long before we even knew who God was. It is a love that transcends all understanding and all boundaries. It is a love that has no limits or conditions. This love is so great that God sent His only Son to die for us, to redeem us, to save us from our sins.

Despite our sinful nature, God loves us anyway. He knows us for who we truly are, with all our faults and imperfections, yet He still loves us. We can't earn this love, nor can we do anything to lose it. It's a love that's freely given by God, out of His own character, not ours.

When we put our faith in Jesus as our Savior, we are saved by His grace, not by our own merits. It's not about what we have done or what we can do, but it's about what Jesus has done for us. We are saved by His sacrifice on the cross, and we are forgiven by His love.

So let us approach God with confidence, knowing that we are loved and accepted by Him. Let us pour out our hearts before Him, confess our sins, and trust that He hears us and loves us. We can thank God for His ever-present love, for His protection, and for the times when He has fought for us. We can thank Him for loving us despite our faults and failures.

We must be vigilant and not allow the familiar lies to convince us that we are alone. Instead, let us seek God's reassurance in His Word and trust in Him today. God wants to fill our hearts with joy and our lives with great happiness. Let us put our trust in Him and know that *nothing* can ever separate us from His love!

> **PRAYER**
>
> *Jesus, I praise You, my Savior and Redeemer. Who is like You, who descended to conquer death and then ascended to the right hand of the Father in heaven? I worship You, for Your love knows no bounds. There is no power that can keep You away from me. You move mountains to be with me! You leave the ninety-nine to find me when I am lost. I praise You, for You are the good Shepherd of my soul. Amen.*

Our Covenant-Keeping God

"The mountains may disappear,
and the hills may come to an end,
but My love will never disappear;
My promises of peace will not come to an end,"
says the LORD, who shows mercy to you.

ISAIAH 54:10 NCV

God's love is the foundation of our faith. It is the cornerstone on which our relationship with Him is built. Our God is covenant-keeping, meaning everything He promises to do He does! God has promised to love us forever, and His love is irrevocable. It is not based on our circumstances or the physical world around us. God's love is eternal. It is not bound by time or space. God has established an unbreakable bond with us, and nothing can separate us from His love. His love is not dependent on our actions or behavior. He loves us because we are His children, and His love for us is unconditional.

The Lord has promised to love us and to have a relationship with us. His love for us is not just a feeling or an emotion; it is a commitment that He has made to us. He desires to be kind toward us, to give us peace, steady our weak knees, and give us rest. His promise of love and relationship will never be broken. He will always be there for us, no matter what we are going through.

Sometimes we base our lives on things that seem sure and certain, but they are not. Only God can be our rock and our strong tower. No mountain, hill, or fortress will ever be more trustworthy than His love for us. We need to trust in God's promises and rely on Him to guide us through life. He will never lead us astray.

God never said we would never be lonely—but we do not need to be discouraged, for God has promised that He will always welcome us. The Holy Spirit is on our side, and He wants to help us. We need to be bold and ask Him for help. We need to ask Him to speak to us through God's Word, to help us understand and process the Bible when we read it, and to help us trust in His promises for us.

God has good things planned for your life! You need to trust in Him, in the power and promises of His Word. Remember that God is in your corner, cheering for you. Trust in His goodness, even when you don't understand what is happening here on earth. He is always with you!

PRAYER

I praise You, God, for You are not a man that You should lie. All Your words are true, and You never go back on Your promises. I worship You, for You are a God of true covenant, and my righteousness is found in You. Lord, You relentlessly pursue me, and You never give me up. I adore You, King of my heart. Amen.

Receiving Hope

And this hope will not lead to disappointment.
For we know how dearly God loves us,
because He has given us the Holy Spirit
to fill our hearts with His love.

ROMANS 5:5 NLT

As we navigate through life, we often find ourselves in situations where we feel lost, alone, and hopeless. However, as believers, we have been given a gift that enables us to experience hope in the midst of any circumstance. That gift is the Holy Spirit.

When Jesus ascended into heaven, He promised His disciples they would not be left alone. He promised to send the Holy Spirit to be their Comforter and Guide. This same promise extends to us today. Through the Holy Spirit, we have access to God's love, peace, and guidance.

The Holy Spirit is not only a gift, but He is also a guarantee of our salvation. It is through the Holy Spirit that we experience the love of God and the hope of our salvation. We can have confidence that God's love for us will never end and that we will one day be united with Him in heaven.

As we put our trust in the Holy Spirit, we can experience freedom from anxiety and fear. We can walk confidently in the knowledge that God is with us, guiding us every step of the way. When we feel overwhelmed, we can turn to the Holy Spirit for peace and strength.

Today, take a moment to thank God for the gift of the Holy Spirit. Remember His faithfulness and love toward you. May you trust in Him and allow the Holy Spirit to guide you as you walk through this life. Lean into His presence and experience the hope that only He can give. Remember that His hope will never disappoint you because God has poured out His love to fill your heart.

PRAYER

Thank You, Holy Spirit, for always being with me. Your comfort and consolation upholds me at all times. I worship You, God, for You have plans for me, plans for a hope and a future, plans for good and not for harm. I exalt You, for You are the great, mighty, and awesome God. My trust is safe when I place it in You. You will never let me down. Amen.

Never Alone

> Jesus said, "Teach these new disciples
> to obey all the commands I have given you.
> And be sure of this: I am with you always,
> even to the end of the age."
>
> **MATTHEW 28:20 NLT**

As we go through the ups and downs of life, it can be easy to feel like we are alone. We may feel as though no one understands what we are going through, or that we are facing challenges that are too difficult to overcome. But as believers, we have a powerful promise to hold on to: that God will be with us forever.

No matter what we face, we are never alone. God's love is a constant that will never change. He is with us through the good and the bad, the happy and the sad. He formed us, and He will be with us until the end of our days. We can take comfort in the fact that God's love has no limits and that there is no expiration date on our time with Him.

We can trust in the knowledge that God will never leave us. Even when we feel like we have turned our backs on Him, He is there, waiting for us to turn back to Him. He is a God of second chances, and His love for us is relentless. He is zealous for us and will never stop pursuing us.

In times of trouble and despair, we can lean on the Holy Spirit for comfort and guidance. We can ask God to give us the faith to trust in His care for us and to believe His promises. When we feel alone, we can remember that God is present and listening to us. He cares for us more than we could ever imagine!

So, give thanks to God for His steadfast loyalty and for the way He cares for us and our families. Let us trust in Him and not waste our time on worry. He is with us always, and His love promises to stay by our side forever. Let us be confident in Him, knowing that He will never leave us!

PRAYER

O God, what are people, that You are mindful of us? And yet Your thoughts of me are more than the sand on the seashore. I praise You, for You outlast time and space. You endure beyond all created things. I worship You, Creator and Crafter of all my days. You knew me before I existed, You chose me before I knew You, and You have prepared a place for me at Your side. I exalt You for Your great steadfastness toward me. No one will ever care for me as You do, Lord. Amen.

SECTION:
ENJOYING LIFE

God Has Good Things for You!

> I remain confident of this:
> I will see the goodness of the Lord
> in the land of the living.
>
> **PSALM 27:13 NIV**

As humans, we often focus on what we lack instead of the abundance around us. It is easy to become fixated on what we don't have, rather than what we do. However, when we shift our focus to the promises of God, we can find hope and peace in the midst of hardship.

God has promised us goodness, not just in heaven, but here on earth, in the "land of the living." He wants us to experience His goodness with our own eyes, and to trust in His promises. It's important to remember that even when we experience pain and hardship, God is with us, and He wants us to experience His joy.

Jesus told us that we would face trials and tribulations, but that we should take heart because He has overcome the world. This means that no matter what we face, we can have hope in our faith and trust that God will keep His promises. Even when circumstances seem dire and all seems lost, we can still hope against hope, knowing that Jesus is in control and that He will come through for us.

In times of doubt or hardship, it's important to take a few minutes to dwell on the promises of God. We can thank Jesus for the good and encouraging words He has spoken over us and thank

God for His faithfulness. We can also think about past situations in which we were overwhelmed with blessings, and thank God for filling our cups to overflowing.

Jesus is the Word of God, the fulfillment of all of God's promises. He has gone ahead to prepare a place for us, but we don't have to wait until we get to heaven to experience God's goodness. We can ask Him to help us see His blessings all around us and ask the Holy Spirit for the ability to experience fullness of joy.

We should expect to see God's goodness here on the earth! We can give ourselves permission to hope and believe that God has beauty and joy for us here. We can open our eyes to the wonders He has placed around us and taste and see that the Lord is good. He has great things in store for us—just wait and see!

PRAYER

Jesus, You are my good Shepherd! You pour out Your blessings upon me, and Your mercies never cease. You overwhelm me with Your kindness and Your goodness. I worship You, for all things are under Your dominion. I adore You, high King of heaven and earth. You have prepared my eyes to see Your wonderful works. Amen.

Keeping Priorities Straight

Take delight in the Lord,
and He will give you your heart's desires.

PSALM 37:4 NLT

As we navigate through life, we sometimes get caught up in pursuing the things we desire. We get so focused on what we want that we forget to appreciate the One who provides it all. God is the Giver of all good gifts, but sometimes we put the gifts above the Giver.

God is the Source of all the blessings we receive. If we seek Him first, everything else will fall into place. We must prioritize God in our lives and give Him preeminence in all things. When we seek God for His own sake, because we love Him, and not just for what He can give us, our lives will be transformed. We will be filled with joy and peace, and our hearts will be aligned with God's will for us.

God already knows the desires of our hearts, but He delights in hearing us call out to Him. He wants us to come before Him, confess our sins, and thank Him for all the blessings He has given us. When we take time to reflect on the past seasons of growth, moments of victory, joy, and new beginnings, we can see how God has been working in our lives. We can thank Him for delighting in us, for partaking in our pleasure, and for every blessing we receive, great and small.

God has great joy in store for us. We can ask Him to fill us with expectation, hope, and endurance. We can choose to seek God every day and know He has wonderful things planned for our lives.

Prioritize God in your life and give Him first place in your heart. As you seek Him, He will provide you with everything you need. Rejoice in serving God every day and enjoy the hope and future He has planned for you!

PRAYER

Heavenly Father, I praise You, for You are my portion on the earth. You satisfy my soul and satiate my spirit. There is nothing I will ever need that You cannot provide. I worship You, Jesus, for You died so that I might have life abundantly. You don't give of Yourself sparingly, but You provide more than enough for me. I exalt You, for You are a good Father and You hold my life in the palm of Your hand. Amen.

Overtaken with Blessings

*You prepare a feast for me
in the presence of my enemies.
You honor me by anointing my head with oil.
My cup overflows with blessings.*

PSALM 23:5 NLT

Provision. It's something we can't live without. We strive for it, work hard for it, and sometimes even worry about it. But we serve a God who is the very embodiment of provision. He doesn't just provide for our basic needs, but He desires to overflow our lives with blessings that we cannot even fathom.

God has a plan for each one of us, and that plan includes prosperity and abundance. He wants to restore every broken area of our lives and fill us with His joy and goodness. When we walk with Him, we will be constantly reminded of His love and provision, and our hearts will overflow with worship and praise.

It can be easy to get caught up in the struggles of life and forget that God is bigger than any obstacle we may face. He is already clearing the path before us; all we need to do is trust and wait on Him. He has already prepared a table of victory for us, and when we come to Him in faith, we will receive all that He has for us.

Take a moment today to reflect on the abundance of God in your life. Thank Him for His love, which cannot be measured, and for His care in providing for all your needs. Ask God to change your mindset and show you what is possible when you expect the extraordinary. You serve a God who is bigger than anything you could ask or imagine, and He wants you to live a life of supernatural abundance!

God's plans for us are greater than we could ever imagine. He wants us to live as overcomers, to be filled with His blessings and goodness. So let's commit to trusting in His provision, to living a life of fullness that overflows with praise to His name!

PRAYER

God, I praise You, for You are always with me. Though I walk through the valley of the shadow of death, You go before me and behind me. You hem me in on every side. Jesus, Your salvation is too wonderful for me to comprehend. You overwhelm me with Your goodness, and You confound me with Your kindness. I worship You, for You are the good Shepherd of my soul. There is no one like You in all the earth! Amen.

Living a Prosperous Life

*Honor the LORD with your wealth
and with the best part of everything you produce.
Then He will fill your barns with grain,
and your vats will overflow with good wine.*

PROVERBS 3:9-10 NLT

Prosperity is a topic that is often debated among Christians. Some believe that God wants us to be prosperous in all areas of our lives, while others believe our focus should be on spiritual prosperity rather than material gain. However, the truth is that God does desire for us to experience blessings.

Jesus said that where our treasure is, there our hearts will be also. Money is necessary to navigate life in modern society, but we must not allow the pursuit of it to rule our hearts and minds. Our focus should be on storing up treasures in heaven, where they cannot be destroyed by moth or rust. We are also called to use our material resources here on earth to grow God's Kingdom. This includes giving offerings and tithes to the Lord.

Abraham and Jacob both gave a tenth of their resources to God, and we are called to do the same. By giving our first and best to the Lord, we show Him that He has first place in our hearts. If we honor God with our tithes and offerings, then our hearts are more aligned with His heart, freeing us from the love of money.

It is important to thank God for His provision and ask Him to confirm His plans for us. We should also ask for faithfulness when He blesses us so we never value the gifts above the Giver. The Holy Spirit can help us hold all that God gives us with open hands.

As you prioritize God's place in your heart above that of money and you honor Him with your tithes and offerings, you will experience His blessings, whatever they look like. Thank God today for His prosperity and always seek to use your material resources to grow His Kingdom on the earth.

PRAYER

God, I worship You, for You are my portion on the earth. Jesus, You died so that I might have life and live more abundantly. You are the God of more than enough. You have more for me than I could ask or think. Your arm is powerful, and Your hand works wonders in our midst. I praise You, for there is no God like You who moves on behalf of His people. Jesus, I exalt You, my Redeemer and Savior. I worship You, for You are a faithful God. Amen.

Safe and Protected

The LORD keeps you from all harm
and watches over your life.
The LORD keeps watch over you
as you come and go, both now and forever.

PSALM 121:7–8 NLT

Protection is something we all long for in life. We want to feel safe and secure in our surroundings, and we want to know we are protected from harm. As believers, we have the promise of God's protection, and this is something we can hold on to in times of trouble.

The Lord is our stronghold and our fortress, and we do not have to fear the terrors of the night or the arrows that fly by day. We can trust in the Lord's protection, knowing that He will preserve our souls. Jesus promised us that we would have trials in this life, but if we put our trust in the Holy Spirit, He will see us through our tribulations.

God has restoration, healing, and joy planned for us. He wants us to run to the shelter of His wings and look to Him for help. He will not forsake us; the Holy Spirit is with us at all times. We need only be still and submit ourselves to His hands, lifting up our eyes to Him and receiving His help.

God is present and listening to us, and He wants to guard our steps and keep us safe. We can ask Him for discernment from the Holy Spirit and for the ability to clearly hear His voice when He warns us. We can ask Him to help us submit to His leading.

The Lord will guard us from all dangers. He will guard us as we come and go, now and forever. He wants to keep us from injury and defeat, and He promised that He would always care and provide for us. So let us trust Him to do just that. May we find our protection in God, our fortress and stronghold, and rest in the assurance of His care for us.

PRAYER

Heavenly Father, I worship You, for You are my help in times of need. I worship You, for You keep my feet from stumbling and my knees from faltering. You uphold me with Your righteous right hand. I praise You, for You are with me in my coming and going, when I lie down and when I get up. You are always before me and behind me. You are great and greatly to be praised! Amen.

Run Your Race in Faith

*Whether you eat or drink,
or whatever you do,
do it all for the glory of God.*

I CORINTHIANS 10:31 NLT

Perseverance is a trait that is highly valued in the Christian faith. It is the ability to keep going, to endure and persist even in the face of difficulties, setbacks, and obstacles. As followers of Christ, we are called to persevere in doing everything for God's glory. We must keep our eyes fixed on Him and our hearts focused on His purposes, even when the road ahead seems long and arduous.

Living for God's glory means that our lives are no longer our own. We have been bought with a price, and our calling is to live out that purpose each day of our lives. It is a journey, not a destination. So we should not wait to arrive at some perceived endpoint to honor God. Instead, we live our lives in a way that glorifies Him at every moment.

Perseverance is not just about endurance; it is also about faith. We must run our race with faith, knowing that God is waiting for us and that He will give us our prize. We must trust that those who persevere in God's goodness will obtain a crown and share in His victory. Each step we take, no matter how small, is a triumph in its own right, and we should give glory to God for every moment.

However, perseverance can be hard. Doubt and fear can creep in, and the road can be long and hard. In those moments, we must remember that God remains faithful, even when we are not. He gives us the strength to continue, and He has a beautiful plan for our lives. We must keep our eyes fixed on Him and ask Him to sustain us in the desert and provide refreshment in dry seasons.

Finally, we remember that everything we do, whether we eat or drink or anything else, it should be done for the glory of God. We must press on and push through, standing upon the truth of His Word and receiving His mighty strength within our souls. So let us be encouraged and continue toward what's ahead, knowing that God has pleasant and amazing plans in store for us.

PRAYER

I praise You, Jesus, for You have called me to do great things, to work for Your Kingdom, and to live life to the fullness of Your goodness. God, I worship You, for You are my joy and my strength. Jesus, in You dwells the fullness of God, and You do all for the glory of God the Father. Holy Spirit, I praise You, for You are my constant companion in all that I do. I honor You, God, and I worship You with all my heart, soul, and strength. Amen.

Identity and Purpose

Finally, all of you should be in agreement, understanding each other, loving each other as family, being kind and humble. Do not do wrong to repay a wrong, and do not insult to repay an insult. But repay with a blessing, because you yourselves were called to do this so that you might receive a blessing. The Scripture says, "A person must do these things to enjoy life and to have many happy days. He must not say evil things, and he must not tell lies. He must stop doing evil and do good. He must look for peace and work for it. The Lord sees the good people and listens to their prayers. But the Lord is against those who do evil."

1 PETER 3:8–12 NCV

God has given you an identity and a purpose that is uniquely yours. You were created with a specific calling and works prepared ahead of you. God has special things prepared just for you to do.

As you journey through life, remember that God has promised you peace if you love Him and follow His commandments. His ways are good, and all His paths lead to freedom. His law is in place for our well-being, to show us what is right and healthy for us. God's commandments are meant to be a blessing to us.

When we trust God's words over our own, we live a more peaceful and contented life. Take a moment to thank Him for giving you His Word and planning your life out in a beautiful way. Give thanks to Jesus for forming each one of your days before you ever existed. Thank God for hearing your prayers and for sending His blessings down on your life.

God has determined your identity and written out all the days of your life in His book. He is closer to you than you think, and this is your moment to reach out to Him. Ask God to reveal His plans to you, to help you be obedient to them, and for the ability to keep His commandments.

As you walk in the identity, calling, and works that God has created for you, endeavor to live in peace with others, to love them, to be kind and humble. The Lord sees those who follow His commandments and looks to bless them. Trust in God and seek His will for your life. May you be filled with faith in the promises of God and an assurance of the wonderful future to come!

PRAYER

Jesus, I praise You, for You are the perfect example to us here on earth. You are all good, all peace, and all righteousness. I praise You, Jesus, for You alone conquered sin and paid its price. I worship You, God, for You prepared Your plans and purposes for me before I was born. You reserved special works for me to do on the earth. You are a faithful God, and You fulfill Your promises to me. I worship You, for You sent the Living Word ahead of me, Jesus, the Prince of Peace, so that I might see Your goodness in the land of the living. Amen.

Giving Thanks in All Things

Be thankful in all circumstances,
for this is God's will for you who belong to Christ Jesus.

I THESSALONIANS 5:18 NLT

Giving thanks to God is an important aspect of our spiritual journey. It is a way to express our gratitude for all the blessings we have received from Him. When we take time to reflect on the good things in our lives, we realize how very much we have to be thankful for!

The Bible encourages us to give thanks in all circumstances, for this is the will of God in Christ Jesus for us (I Thessalonians 5:18 NIV). This means that even in difficult times, we should find reasons to thank God. When we do this, we shift our focus from our problems to the goodness of God, which helps us to have a better perspective.

Psalm 100:4 says, "Enter his gates with thanksgiving, and his courts with praise! Give thanks to him; bless his name!" (ESV). This verse reminds us that thanksgiving is a way to approach God. When we come to Him with a heart of gratitude, we honor Him and acknowledge His goodness in our lives.

One way to cultivate a spirit of thanksgiving is to keep a gratitude journal. This is a journal in which you write down things you are thankful for each day. It could be as simple as being thankful for a beautiful sunset or a good meal. By doing this, you train your mind to focus on the positive things in your life.

Another way to give thanks is to share your blessings with others. You could do this by volunteering your time or resources to help those in need. When we give to others, we not only bless them, but we also honor God and acknowledge that everything we have comes from Him.

Giving thanks to God should be a daily practice for every believer. It is a way to approach God, cultivate a positive attitude, and honor Him for His goodness in our lives. Let's take time each and every day to reflect on the good things we have received from Him and give Him thanks.

PRAYER

Heavenly Father, I come before You with a heart full of gratitude for all the blessings You have poured into my life. Thank You for the gift of life, for my family and friends, for the food on my table, and for the roof over my head. Thank You, as well, for Your love, grace, and mercy that sustain me every day. I am blessed beyond measure. Amen.

God's Great Love

Jesus said, "For this is how God loved the world:
He gave His one and only Son,
so that everyone who believes in Him will not perish
but have eternal life."

JOHN 3:16 NLT

The love of God is a powerful force that transcends all boundaries and limitations. It is a love that is unconditional and never fails. The Bible says in I John 4:8 that "God is love." This means that everything that God does is motivated by love.

God's love for us is demonstrated in many ways. The most profound demonstration of His love came through the sacrifice of His Son, Jesus Christ. John 3:16 says, "For God so loved the world that He gave His one and only Son, that whoever believes in Him shall not perish but have eternal life" (NIV). This verse shows us that God's love is not just an abstract concept, but it is something that has been put into action.

God's love for us is not based on our performance or our good deeds. It is a love that is freely given to us, regardless of who we are or what we have done. Romans 5:8 says, "But God demonstrates His own love for us in this: While we were still sinners, Christ died for us" (NIV). This means that even when we were at our worst, God loved us enough to send His Son to die for us.

God's love for us is also everlasting. Jeremiah 31:3 says, "I have loved you with an everlasting love; I have drawn you with unfailing kindness" (NIV). This means that God's love for us will never end, and it will never fail. No matter what we do, God will always love us.

As you consider the love of God, be filled with gratitude and awe. You can be thankful for the sacrifice that God made for you, as well as amazed that He loves each of us so much. May this love motivate us to love others with the same kind of love that God has shown us. In I John 4:11, we are commanded to love one another, because God has loved us.

The love of God is a powerful force that transforms us from the inside out. It is a love that is unconditional, everlasting, and never fails. As we seek to grow in our relationship with God, let us always remember the love that He has shown us, and let us strive to love others with the same kind of love.

PRAYER

Dear heavenly Father, I thank You for Your goodness and love, which have sustained me throughout life's ups and downs. Your grace has brought me this far, and Your mercy has kept me safe. I look forward to walking through the rest of my life with You by my side and spending all of eternity in Your wonderful presence in heaven. Amen.

ABOUT PRAY.COM

Pray.com serves millions of Christians worldwide with powerful and life-changing messages, prayers, podcasts, and meditations. Following the success of the audio plan, *Morning Gratitude*, *Morning Gratitude: Inspiring Moments to Start Your Day* is designed to help you step into a serene and focused space.

Pray.com is driven by a mission to grow faith and cultivate community. Pray.com makes prayer a priority by bringing people world-class messages, daily devotions, and Bible stories narrated by inspirational celebrities, athletes, and authors.

Learn more about Pray.com and gain access to their unique content geared toward strengthening your walk with God by scanning the QR code!